Sacred COWS

a Lighthearted Look at Belief and Tradition Around the World

Seth Andrews

Illustrations by Vincent Deporter
Foreword by Brian Dalton

outskirtspress
DENVER, COLORADO

MW01291951

Acknowledgements

Authors, artists and producers are familiar with the sine wave of the creative process. It's a thrill ride of peaks and valleys which (at least for me) follows this progression:

STAGE 1: "What a great idea!"
STAGE 2: "These first pieces are coming along nicely."
STAGE 3: "Wow. This is a much bigger project than I realized."
STAGE 4: "Meh."
STAGE 5: "My cerebrum is a dry, rocky place. Inspiration is lost. I can't feel my legs."
STAGE 6: "Merciful death, take me."
STAGE 7: "Maybe I'll get lucky, and it won't suck."
STAGE 8: "On the horizon...a white light."
STAGE 9: "Finished!"
STAGE 10: {conspicuous alcohol consumption}

Along the way, there have been key people who helped me, supported me, inspired me and kept me from careening off the tracks and into a retaining wall, and I'd be remiss if I didn't take a moment to acknowledge them.

As his contribution has been so valuable, I must bow down and pay tribute to the tremendous talents of my illustrator for this book,

i

Vincent Deporter, who has drawn for SpongeBob SquarePants, Scooby Doo, DC Comics, the Nickelodeon network and much more. I had been searching for an artist who could crawl into my skull and capture the fun, funny, interesting and occasionally irreverent illustrations I'd envisioned. Vince took my meager ideas, packed them in his creative rocket ship and blasted into the stratosphere. As we neared the book's completion, I'd check in for Vince's latest updates, and each newly-uploaded image would make me smile (and occasionally laugh out loud). I have little doubt that the response of the reader will be much the same. The text may be the meat of "Sacred Cows," but the artwork has added the spice. Thanks, Vincent, for allowing us to enjoy your amazing gift, and for helping this humble author realize a dream.

I must also thank Hilary Sadhoo for her friendship, for her invaluable help in the research for this book, and for standing among that small, select ilk of attorneys that isn't comprised of obnoxious douchenozzles. At key points over the years, she has happily stepped in to do some rather unglamorous legwork on my behalf, and whether she's poring over papers or holding a camera in a winter's snow, she displays an almost obscene amount of goodwill and good cheer. Thanks, Hilary, for your sharp eye and contagious enthusiasm.

As I hammered this book into submission, I also relied on others who were kind enough to lend their time and perspective when I had questions or needed another set of eyes: Tony Ortega, David Fitzgerald, Shelly Rau, James Underdown and Edward Tarte.

And finally, my wife Natalie has spent many days and nights as both a bemused spectator and strong supporter of my endeavors. It's not uncommon for me to be up to my neck in a book chapter, preparation for the next radio show or some ambitious video production, and she (usually) patiently understands that "just ten more minutes" means that I'm terrified of breaking a creative rhythm and might not actually emerge until the next full moon. She has been my sounding board, my test audience, my motivational coach and the great equalizer. Balance is often difficult for producers, and Natalie has been there as a reminder that life exists outside of the deadlines, that a real sunset is much more satisfying than a Windows screensaver, and that all work and no play makes Seth a dull boy. Yeah, she thinks I'm insane, but she loves me anyway, and that makes me a very lucky guy.

Foreword

by Brian Dalton

There are very few things or people I hate more than Seth Andrews. I hate unnecessarily difficult packaging, stubbing my infant toe on the corner of the bed in the middle of the night, an adult using the word "gross" on national television as though he were thirteen, and people who hog the passing lane without regret. After that, the list is very short: Seth, Seth, and more Seth.

Those who know him well tell me there is even more to hate. But I do not walk in those circles. My hatred is nurtured from afar, where I find myself compelled to watch his videos and listen to his podcasts.

Is it blind jealousy? Perhaps. But most annoying of all is his ability to interrupt my sleep as I obsess over the intrinsic unfairness of the universe and try to figure out where the Hell Seth finds the time to do everything he does.

First, let's talk about those pipes. How unfair is it that Seth is gifted with a voice that makes James Earl Jones -not to be confused with James Earl Ray- feel bad about himself (and not just for his ill-advised association with CNN)? Seth speaks in round, smooth, booming tones. By comparison, I fear that I sound like the squeaks of a distressed dolphin. This loathing of Seth and his "lullaby larynx" is deepened every time a telemarketer calls me ma'am.

Then there are the fantastic videos he creates as a professional producer and YouTube host (videos which, again, often feature that voice). Being in the "biz" myself, I am genuinely in awe of these productions. Where does he find the inspiration, the insight, the time? Has Seth somehow managed to secretly clone himself? Did he win the lottery, enabling him to afford an army of video editors and animators? These are the questions that keep me up at night.

One of my favorite insights in Seth's videos came from his piece, "The Story of Creation," which pondered the question of why God created humankind to be completely naked. Obviously, there's the awkwardness of the whole thing, made even more uncomfortable (and impractical) by having one's "private bits" exposed so publicly to sharp edges and harsh climates. With his satirical eye toward the Garden of Eden, Seth managed to key in on the fact that virtually everything in Adam's world would be a source of abrasion, and a serious hazard for his bared bologna. The whole scenario does make one wonder if God really sat back and thought things through. This is a frequent theme he and I both enjoy skewering — the obvious and ever-present lack of intelligence in this supposedly "intelligent design."

Of course, my sleep is further hindered by his wonderful radio podcast, as I am again forced to ask, "Are there hours in the day that I just don't know about?" He's got that super cool opening with the four horsemen that makes him sound totally legit. He has great guests. Great questions. Hell, he even has sponsorship! What the heck is this guy doing that I'm not? It's infuriating!!!

And now, piling on top of all that, Seth has a book. Of course he does.

God forbid he should leave a medium untouched — or for the rest of us!

Of course, when he sent me the text to look over, suggesting that maybe I could write the Foreword (an honor, by the way), I agreed because I couldn't imagine he'd have the time to do an equally good job in print. I've written quite a bit in my life, and I know that writing is not something that most do well, with ease, or without having a good deal of secluded, quiet time. With the videos, the animation, the production, the voice-overs, the interviews, the podcast, etc, I simply couldn't imagine it. I would finally be able to sleep knowing that there's something Seth Andrews does poorly.

Fortunately for you, I have been foiled again. *Sacred Cows* is a highly entertaining and informative mish-mash of humor and heart, displaying for all to see the skills of a true communicator...skills which will only further my hatred and jealousy. Seth has managed to be witty, clever, and insightful. Heck, he even shows an ability to use proper punctuation and spelling — a rare find in the texting era.

Sacred Cows is a delight. There. I said it. You happy? Now, if you'll forgive me, I need a nap!

Brian Dalton
Actor, Director
"Mr. Deity" / "The Way of the Mister"

Introduction

I'm sometimes asked if I believe that intelligent life exists beyond earth.

A serious answer to this question would more appropriately come from a Neil deGrasse Tyson type, but I can't help but look up at the sky and think that a universe populated with hundreds of billions of galaxies would probably have at least ONE other life form smart enough to invent the screwdriver.

In fact, the idea that humankind might represent the full potential of evolutionary biology frightens me, as our species seems to have some kind of brain parasite that makes us more interested in designer jeans and cat videos than world peace, missions to Saturn and the decoded human genome.

I imagine an extraterrestrial peering through the cosmos, looking down (yeah, I know there's not a "down" in space) and observing us like Sir David Attenborough might observe a colony of termites. If such an alien were to witness the cauldron of unusual, sometimes violent and often ridiculous human behavior found on every continent, I fear it would slap its forehead and make immediate plans to fumigate.

And why not? We're humans...and humans are ridiculous.

To be fair, we've got our highlight reel, and we rightfully swell with pride at our greatest moments and grandest achievements: Neil Armstrong's footprint on the surface of the moon. Edmund Hillary and Tenzing Norgay blazing a trail to the peak of Mount Everest. The writings of Mark Twain. The harnessing of electricity. The building of the Pyramids. The artificial heart. The symphony orchestra. Sky scrapers. Philosophy. The civil rights movement. Da Vinci's Mona Lisa. The automobile. The internet. Vaccines. The potato cannon. Thin mints. Etc.

And even in less conspicuous instances, our species does provide a great many examples of benevolent, mature and forward-thinking behavior worthy of tribute. Men, women and youth of all shapes, sizes, colors, cultures and creeds live balanced, rational, reason-based lives, sloughing off all ideas, traditions and practices that might encumber them. These well-rounded poster children for the species make the chest swell with pride.

Unfortunately, it doesn't take long before attention is drawn from the best of us…to the rest of us. Too often, humankind is the lemming walking over the cliff, the car drifting into oncoming traffic, the June bug ramming its head repeatedly into the screen door.

We're like the zombie ants infected with the brain-eating fungus, walking our drone bodies to their doom. We're the lumbering armadillo peering across a busy eight-lane expressway declaring, "I can make it!" We're the reason that there's a hugely popular website called Fail Blog. We're a punch line waiting to be told at parties.

Indeed, at every turn, our species defines itself with illogical, bizarre and often destructive behavior more worthy of Mad Magazine than the Smithsonian, at least in the eyes of this humble observer. And that's what I am - a humble observer. I'm an everyman peering around at his earthly kin with genuine curiosity, good humor, frequent concern and often jaw-dropping disbelief. I'm the tourist snapping photos for the local paper, or the shell-shocked journalist scribbling notes from the foxhole, or even the family dog sticking his head out of the car so he can bark at a dead skunk.

If you're looking for a history book, this ain't it. If you're seeking the keen analysis of a trained anthropologist, keep looking. If you crave deep understanding of belief in relation to human psychology, immediately contact the retailer, get your money back, and find the appropriate category at your nearest bookstore.

However, if you're up for a short trip around the planet with a layman tour guide who is also an enthusiastic spectator, place your seatback in the upright and locked position.

For better or for worse, this book is a conduit so that others can see this crazy world through my eyes. It's a flashy pinball machine that seeks, above all, to entertain, and while you and I are being amused, perhaps we can rack up a few points. Throughout this (incredibly random) journey across geography, humanity, culture and tradition, it's my hope that we'll learn some things about each other, find plenty of opportunities for laughter, bond a bit as friends and ultimately encourage each other to do a double-take on many of the cherished beliefs and traditions we may have previously insulated from challenge.

Will many of my observations speak to the traditions and doctrines of religions? Absolutely. But if any of these chapters nip at the heels of the sacred cows in your own life, I hope you'll see them for what they are: perspectives. Any omnipotent deities will be unconcerned about the writings of this humble scribe, and any worthy traditions will certainly survive my jabs. After all, a steadfast castle will outlast the stones tossed by a single foot soldier, and if the structure does begin to crumble, a weak and unworthy fortress will be revealed. It's a win-win. And it'll be fun!

We'll address the Church of Euthanasia, penis parades, magic underwear, psychic foot readings, Tibetan sky burials, Jediism, self-crucifixion, snake handlers, wish cows, giraffe women, Christmas demons and more, and we'll take a fresh look at some of the more mainstream beliefs and practices that, seen with an objective eye, rank right up there with baby tossing and astral travel.

So don the tin foil hat and toast your communion glass to these random explorations of humankind's wildest and weirdest, and try to finish before the Great Galactic Boot comes to squash us out of our misery.

CHAPTER 1
Once Bitten

I know it sounds strange, but I feel sorry for snakes. They're forced to watch as you and I fawn, giggle and coo at their fluffier, cuter counterparts. Tweet a photograph of a bunny, a monkey, a meerkat or even a baby porcupine, and you'd think your friends were gushing at a baby shower. Follow it up with a snake, and a long chain of snake horror stories will materialize almost instantly. "I found a snake in my shoe." "I killed a snake in the yard." "I heard about someone's pet snake crawling into his bed, coiling around his neck and decapitating him!"

A lot of people out there suffer from Ophidiophobia[1] (the fear of snakes), and I totally get it. There's something about the sleek, almost sinister line of the serpent. The scales. The darkly intelligent and never-closing eyes. The arrow-shaped head. The sssssssmiling mouth. And of course, inside the mouth of the poisonous snake, a venom-filled syringe of doom.

It's this fear that explains the vast library of snake-based horror films out there. (Check out "Piranhaconda" on SyFy. It's a classic.) It explains how even the tiniest of garden snakes can shut down a house party. And, apparently, our fear of snakes has an evolutionary origin.

---

1   "Ophidiophobia, n." *Merriam Webster Medical Dictionary Online*. Encyclopedia Britannica, 2015. Web.

In a study helmed by Michael J. Penkunas and Richard G. Coss at the University of California's Department of Psychology, it was discovered that the mere sight of a legless reptile triggers a natural fear mechanism in the primate brain, apparently a holdover from a distant past when snakes posed a significant threat to our survival.[2]

A 2009 study in Japan revealed that monkeys responded to images of snakes faster than other, happier images (flowers, etc), despite the fact that *none of the monkeys had ever actually seen a snake before.*[3] They, like human beings, had simply evolved a natural instinct to freak out and jump onto the couch.

Neuroscientists in Brazil and Japan recently tested a "Snake Detection Theory," which was posed in 2007 by anthropologist Lynne A. Isbell,[4] examining a region of the brain called the pulvinar. Neurons in the pulvinar apparently receive signals from the eyes and direct our attention quickly to specific objects within our field of view. If our visual picture is populated with a yard, a road, a gate, a sunset, a lawn chair and a snake, the snake will almost immediately become our primary focus, and this quick recognition has been a critical element of human survival. In fact, we should probably be thanking the snake, because if Professor Isbell's data is correct, it is a primary reason that we higher primates have superior vision and larger brains. Snakes…made us smarter.

Actually, snakes made *some* of us smarter. There is a church culture that instructs the faithful to not only ignore their panicky pulvinar, but to actually invite poisonous snakes into their homes and

---

2   Zimmer, Carl. "Afraid of Snakes? Your Pulvinar May Be to Blame". *New York Times*. 31 October 2013. Web.

3   Shibasaki, Masahiro; Kawai, Nobuyuki. "Rapid detection of snakes by Japanese monkeys (Macaca fuscata): An evolutionarily predisposed visual system". *Journal of Comparative Psychology*. Vol 123(2), May 2009, 131-135. Web.

4   Hamilton, John. "Eeek, Snake! Your Brain Has A Special Corner Just For Them". *National Public Radio*. 28 October 2013, 3:45pm ET. Web.

churches for a Sunday morning snack. These wild, weird, pulpit-pounding Pentecostals are called "snake handlers," and you haven't lived until you've seen footage of their antics on YouTube.

Scattered throughout Alabama, Kentucky, South Carolina, Tennessee and West Virginia, an estimated 125 snake-handling churches take literally the words of Mark 16:18, "They shall take up serpents; and if they drink any deadly thing, it shall not hurt them; they shall lay hands on the sick, and they shall recover."[5]

Except when they don't.

At regular intervals, news reports surface about some poor schlub who was dancin', prayin', flailin' and testifyin' when the venomous copperhead in his hands decided he'd had enough. Fangs went in. Poison came out. And as snakes aren't exactly the most social of creatures, the behavior is understandable. Hell…as a human being, I'm tolerant of crowds and commotion, but I'd probably start recoiling and gnashing if I found myself getting tossed around inside one of these clap traps.

The fascinating part is that after these snake-handlers pluck venomous snakes from under their comfy, warm rocks, cram them into sacks, dump them into cages, drag them into a church building and yank them around like armless puppets, they get snake-bitten and then have the nerve to act SURPRISED!

Pastor Jamie Coots of Middlesboro, Kentucky wasn't just a snake-handling preacher. He was a *famous* snake-handling preacher, starring alongside Pastor Andrew Hamblin in the National Geographic television series, "Snake Salvation," which followed his snake hunts in the Appalachia hills and the handling of poisonous snakes during services

5   Dias, Elizabeth. *"Snake Salvation:* One Way to Pray in Appalachia". *Time*. 9 September 2013. Web.

at the Full Gospel Tabernacle in Jesus' Name.

A third-generation reptile wrangler, Coots believed strongly that he risked eternal hellfire unless he took up the serpent, and his exploits often crossed him with the law. He'd been arrested[6] in 2008 for keeping 74 snakes in his home without a permit, and in February 2013, he was sentenced to a year of probation for illegally entering the state of Tennessee with venomous snakes. (Isn't breaking the law a sin?)

In many cases, anti-snake handling laws (misdemeanors) aren't enforced, as authorities don't want to appear as enemies of religious liberty, despite the fact that many snake handlers apparently mistreat the animals. An October 2013 report by NPR (featuring the opinions of Kentucky Reptile Zoo herpetologists) suggested that the reluctance of many snakes to bite is due to the withholding of food and water. A snake that "may be dehydrated, underweight and sick from close confinement is less likely to strike than a healthy snake."[7] In many cases, malnourishment also dilutes the potency of the venom.

Jamie Coots was alleged to have malnourished snakes in his care, and he admitted to NPR that his snakes usually only lived three or four months instead of the usual 10-20 years observed in other captivity environments, brushing away criticism as an attempt to "discredit" God's good work.

Coots first attracted national attention back in the mid '90s when he and a snake-handling buddy named John Wayne "Punkin" Brown were featured in a best-selling book titled, "Salvation on Sand Mountain: Snake Handling and Redemption in Southern Appalachia." Ironically,

---

6   *Smoke 'Em Out.* "Snake Salvation". National Geographic. Original air date 10 September 2013. Web.

7   Burnett, John. "Serpent Experts Try To Demystify Pentecostal Snake Handling". *National Public Radio.* 18 October 2013, 4:12pm ET. Web.

Brown died in 1998. Of snakebite. Brown's wife had died by snakebite a few years earlier. Their five children were handed over to the grandparents living in Tennessee who were also snake-handlers.[8] Out of the frying pan...

But Coots carried on, with the puncture marks to prove it, having been bitten no less than nine times over 22 years, including one incident which cost him the middle finger on his right hand.[9] (Refusing medical treatment, he simply let the snake's poison go unchecked, and the rotted flesh ultimately exposed a quarter inch of bone before the top part of the finger finally broke off.[10] Ick.)

On the night of Saturday, February 15th, 2014, Jamie Coots' luck finally ran out, as the rattlesnake bite to his right hand proved fatal. His family refused medical treatment when paramedics arrived (snake handlers believe the life/death decision is God's alone), and the toxic venom did its work. Coots drew his last breath at home while lying in his favorite chair.

8   Breed, Allen G. "Custody Fight for Snake Handlers' Orphans Pits Faith Against Safety". *Los Angeles Times*. 13 December 1998. Web.
9   Burnett, John. "For Snake-Handling Preacher, 10th Bite Proves Fatal". *National Public Radio*. 17 February 2014, 4:00pm ET. Web.
10   Ross, Phillip. "'Snake Salvation' Star Jamie Coots Dies From Snake Bite After Kentucky Pastor Refuses Treatment In Name Of God". *International Business Times*. 16 February 2014. Web.

Of course, stories like this are red meat for the Nancy Grace crowd, and within hours, this tiny Sunday-to-go-meetin' church house in Middlesboro was the subject of world attention. News reports popped up in the New York Times, USA Today, the Huffington Post, and even the Wall Street Journal. Social media pages saw a huge spike in traffic. Debate raged about the validity of snake-handling as a demonstration of faith in God. Some mourned the needless waste of a precious human life. Others declared it just another Darwin Award.

For me, the most interesting part of this story came at the end, when Jamie Coots' son, Cody, declared via social media that he aspired to one day take up his father's mantle and become a snake-handling minister himself. Then...he begged for money (which is the mark of any good preacher), *because his father hadn't carried a life insurance policy, and the family had no money!*[11]

OK. Let's recap.

- Someone did something incredibly stupid.

- It backfired.

- Total strangers were asked to subsidize the stupidity.

- It was openly announced that the stupidity would continue.

Is this not like asking the neighbors to pay for a new house after you burn the first one down in a meth explosion? It makes no sense! In fact, the entire snake-handling culture comes off as freakish and surreal, aptly described in Thomas Burton's 1993 book, "Serpent Handling Believers:"[12]

---

11   The Coots Family. "In Memory of Bro. Jamie Coots and support for his family". *Facebook*. 16 February 2014. Web.
12   Burton, Thomas. *Serpent Handling Believers*. Knoxville, TN: University of Tennessee Press, 1993. Print.

"Since most of us tend to seek simple, concrete explanations for phenomena, it is easy to view one aspect of serpent handling rather than the whole and, consequently, either to romanticize or brutalize the people and the practice. One can feel after attending a service that it is completely irrational, wild people running around, falling down, quivering, uttering strange sounds; drinking deadly poisons; taking venomous serpents (giant and tiny ones, coiled, extended, limp, knotted together, rattlers, cottonmouths, copperheads, cobras) and staring at them nose to nose, wrapping them around their necks, wearing them on their heads, pitching them, carrying armloads of them, shaking them, petting them; displaying arms tattooed with snakes, hands atrophied by bites, fingers missing, clothing embroidered and etched with snakes — or feel the same sense of the bizane after going into homes and seeing live deadly snakes in closets and adjoining rooms, pictures framed on the wall of people with handfuls of rattlers, photo albums of disfigured bodies from venom poisoning, or a huge frozen rattlesnake taken out of a freezer by a relative of a person whom the serpent killed during a funeral service for yet another snakebit victim."

Of course, Jamie Coots' funeral was a single statistic in a long line of them.

 George Went Hensley, founder of Florida's Church of Jesus with Signs Following (alleged to be the very first snake-handling church). He died on July 25, 1955. In his defense, Hensley was illiterate, so perhaps he couldn't read warning signs.[13]

---

13 Kimbrough, David L. *Taking Up Serpents: Snake Handlers of Eastern Kentucky.* Macon, Georgia: Mercer University Press, 2002. Web.

Shirley Wagers of the Pentecostal Holiness Church in Kentucky. He (yes, Shirley was a man) was killed by poisonous snakebite in November of 1973. He was 72.[14]

 Charles Herman Prince of the Apostolic Church of God in Tennessee. He was killed in August of 1985 after the one-two punch of drinking strychnine and then getting attacked by a rattlesnake. He refused medical attention. He didn't live to regret it.[15]

 Reverend Dwayne Long of the Arthurs Chapel Church of Rose Hill, Virginia. He was bitten and killed in April of 2004. Ironically, his death occurred on Resurrection Sunday. [16]

 Pastor Mark "Mack" Wolfard at a May 2012 outdoor service in West Virginia's Panther State Forest. 39 years earlier, Mark's father (also a snake-handling pastor) met the very same fate. Like father, like son.[17]

These are mere drops in the glass. In fact, over sixty cases of death by snakebite in religious services have been documented in the United States, a statistic made even more tragic by the fact that these adherents to Mark 16:17-18 probably don't realize many of the earliest New Testament manuscripts didn't even include those verses. Many bible scholars take the 8th verse as the proper ending of the chapter and book, with Mary Magdalene, Mary the mother of James and Salome finding the empty tomb of Christ and fleeing. The End. (It's widely

---

14   Kimbrough, David L. *Taking Up Serpents: Snake Handlers of Eastern Kentucky*. Macon, Georgia: Mercer University Press, 2002. Web.
15   Associated Press. "Defiant Snake Handler Dies". *New York Times*. 20 August 1985. Web.
16   "Snakebite proves fatal to minister". *Kingsport Times-News*. 15 April 2004. Web.
17   "Snake-handling pastor dies after bite". *The Boston Globe*. 1 June 2012. Web.

believed that verses 9-20 were later added by a different author to include accounts of Jesus' resurrection and miracles, which make for a much more satisfactory cap to the crucifixion story.)[18]

Alas, even here in the 21st century, I have no doubt that the song of the snake-handler will continue, and every year or so, we'll discover in the obituary column yet another snake-smitten sermonizer who chooses prayer over his pulvinar and (literally) gives up the ghost.

---

18   Carrier, Richard. *"Hitler Homer Bible Christ: The Historical Papers of Richard Carrier 1995-2013"* Ch. 16. Print.

CHAPTER 2
Air Supply

An acquaintance of mine had a dog named "Dexter." A smart and affable Chinese pug, Dexter had only been taught a single trick: He would roll over in exchange for a treat. One needed only to give the verbal command, and the dog would barrel roll, pop up to a standing position and receive his reward.

It was cute at first. But then Dexter apparently decided that he could conjure snacks from his masters by rolling without any command. So as we sat on the couch in front of the television or grazed the hors d'oeuvres at the bar, Dexter could often be seen spinning across the floor like he'd been booted off the top of a steep hill. He rolled and rolled and rolled, because after all, that's when the goodies appear.

It may be difficult to believe, but there are tribes on the island of Tanna, Vanuatu in the South Pacific that, like Dexter, are performing a specific trick in the hopes that treats will fall from the sky.

Let's start at the beginning...with a figure named John Frum. Like most legends, the story of Frum's origin varies quite a bit (depending on the storyteller), but he's often depicted as a United States soldier in the Second World War, his moniker possibly a variation on "John from America." Other accounts describe Frum as an island native adorned in

western attire (that's western like the nations, not like "Gunsmoke"). Still others insist that John Frum was an agent of the spirit world, a ghost, a god. A few legends link him to John the Baptist.

There's no compelling evidence for a literal John Frum, but a religion has blossomed around his name. The popular version of the story goes like this:

The islands had been colonized by the British and French. Strict Christian missionaries stepped onto native soil and immediately outlawed the sacred and beloved traditions of the indigenous Melanesian people. No more dancing. No more polygamy. No more smoking and sacrificing to honor deities and spirits that couldn't be found in the Christian bible. These religious colonizers marched into Tanna like

Dana Carvey's church lady might march onto Daytona Beach during Spring Break. One look at that writhing cauldron of hedonistic, heathen debauchery was all it took. The party was over, and the residents of Tanna found themselves living and serving at the pleasure of their new masters, with many natives forced into hard labor.

After decades of living under a European thumb, the oppressed islanders (led by a charismatic figure presumed to be John Frum) rebelled, cast off the European customs, clothing and currency that had been forced upon them, and retreated inland to resume the Old Ways. Frum allegedly promised that the spirits would bless all who participated in this brave escape, and the original (heathen!) rituals again became a prime directive of the tribe. They tossed their money into the ocean. They rejected schooling. They discarded European dresses and pants in favor of grass skirts and penis sheaths. They again performed dances and sacrifices for the pleasure of the spirits, and they focused on little besides eating, sleeping, shagging, making magic, honoring the gods and waiting for their blessings from the sky.[19]

Then, in the 1940s, World War 2 came to the South Pacific, with hundreds of thousands of American troops arriving by sea and by air. These strange westerners, much more congenial than the European interlopers, were announced by large ships and giant airplanes loaded with all manner of supplies: canned foods, bicycles, jeeps, tents, cigarette lighters, cameras, sugar, weapons, kitchen appliances, designer clothing, medicine, etc. They built hospitals. They constructed bridges. They fashioned their huts out of curious metals. They produced and provided marvelous things that the people of Tanna had never before seen. And when a project necessitated labor from the natives, the Americans (gasp!) paid them a wage. It was

---

19   Guiart, Jean. "John Frum Movement in Tanna Oceania" *Southwest Journal of Anthropology*. 1952. Vol. 22 (3). pp. 165–177. Print.

    a.   Attenborough, David. *People of Paradise*. New York: Harper & Brothers. 1960. Print.

the South Pacific equivalent of the Second Coming, and the accompanying windfall was no less than an outpouring of favor from the gods![20]

As Arthur C. Clarke said in his Third Law, "Any sufficiently advanced technology is indistinguishable from magic," and magic was the only explanation these islanders could imagine for the wonders thrust upon them. Where an American soldier might have seen a simple, metal barbecue grill filled with charcoal and beef, a Melanesian quite probably stood agape at that holy cauldron of black firestones and its billows of offertory smoke (no doubt the aroma of sacrificial animal flesh, smothered in its honey barbecue glaze, greatly pleasing the spirits).

The troops brought supplies for themselves. They also brought extra goodies for the locals. With constant sea traffic and the parachuted supply drops of cargo planes, every day was Christmas, every shipment a winning lottery ticket, and the island of Tanna rejoiced in its embarrassment of riches.

Then, the war ended.

After Japan surrendered to the allies in 1945, "John from America" suddenly disappeared back into the sea and sky with his ships, his planes, his cargo pallets, his candy bars and Coca-Cola, his blue jeans, wristwatches, coffee makers, powered vehicles and home appliances. The spirit world was no longer bringing forth its daily blessings. About this, there was much consternation and lamentation, especially after those previous years of plenty. The natives simply didn't understand. Perhaps the gods needed to be appeased.

So, the Melanesians quickly decided to beg the spirits to return these American agents and their material marvels to their shores. To make

---

20   Mercer, Phil. "Cargo Cult Lives on in South Pacific". *BBC News*. 17 February 2007. Web.

the American return more attractive, they worked to recreate the environment which existed during the occupation. The natives built piers for ships. They cleared large fields to create airstrips which emulated those used by the American military. They painted buildings, piers and fences with the Red Cross logo, which had been a common sight as ambulances and medical ships transported and treated the combat-wounded. They built air traffic control towers out of bamboo (complete with headsets fashioned from rope and coconuts), and they walked the runways mimicking the hand signals that once brought American airplanes in for safe landings.

They desperately craved the return of "cargo" from its magical place of origin, and for that reason, these island residents of Tanna became known as a "cargo cult."

Merriam Webster defines "cargo cult" as: *any of various Melanesian religious groups characterized by the belief that material wealth (as money or manufactured goods) can be obtained through ritual worship.* (Material wealth can be obtained through ritual worship? I guess this makes Joel Osteen's church a cargo cult, no?)

Cargo cults popped up in various places for various reasons, but most died out after years of empty skies, the despondent cult followers dragging themselves back to the colossal anti-climax that was their pre-war routine. The signal had been sent, but no reply had been given. It was time to move on.

A few cargo cults exist today, the most famous being the one associated with John Frum, and that movement continues to honor the spirits and petition for blessings with its annual festival: John Frum Day. Once a year, on February 15th, the faithful congregate in Tanna's Sulphur Bay under the shadow of Yasur volcano to conduct a military parade. Cult members dress in American military clothing, fly high the American flag (on a pole fashioned from a nearby tree), march in step with rifles carved out of bamboo, and proudly paint "USA" on their bodies. Flowers are placed upon a red cross (the John Frum movement's most sacred icon) as the spirits are again asked to return the heyday of magical extravagance to the humble shores of Tanna.[21]

It's a curious thing to watch an entire culture lock its eyes on the joys of yesterday. I suppose it's not that uncommon, really. We've all seen the star athlete spend his autumnal years recounting decades-old victories on the field. We've encountered the sad stares of those who climbed to a peak of prominence and prosperity before plummeting into a mist of obscurity and lament. We've heard the tales about the "Glory Days,"

---

21   Raffaele, Paul. "In John They Trust". *Smithsonian Magazine*. February 2006. Web.
      a.   Johanson, Mark. "Who is John Frum? Burning Man 2013's Link To A 'Cargo Cult' in Vanuatu". *International Business Times*. 3 September 2013. Web.

those memories of times past an obsession for those who cannot (or will not) live in the present. And we've all seen examples of those who pin their hopes on the horizon, begging for the fulfillment that they have yet to create for themselves.

Perhaps these cargo cults might learn a thing or two from Dexter. He may have been just a Chinese pug, but it didn't take him long to discover that performing tricks without request or reward was a lousy method for getting what he wanted out of life.

Come to think of it, that's a lesson for the ages. Rolling over and over doesn't make us happy. It only makes us dizzy. And if we'll focus our attention on living life, seeing the world, playing, working, connecting, relaxing, chewing on the good stuff and occasionally getting scratched behind the ears, we just might receive a tasty morsel that we hadn't been expecting.

CHAPTER 3
Blowing Smoke

On March 13th, 2013, North Korea announced it would no longer acknowledge the Korean Armistice Agreement and threatened to annihilate its enemies worldwide. That same day, a twin-engine Embraer 821 crashed in Pará, Brazil, killing ten. Civil war raged in Syria, with a lethal rocket attack near Damascus. Adam Giles was elected to be the new leader of the County Liberal Party in Australia's Northern Territory. Astronomers celebrated the anniversary of William Herschel's 1781 discovery of Uranus. And pockets of the planet celebrated Good Samaritan Day by helping both friend and stranger.

Meanwhile, on that same day, a group called the Papal Conclave (translated: rich virgins in funny hats) huddled in secret to determine who would replace the retiring supreme pontiff, His Holiness Pope Benedict XVI. Indeed, the Pope had officially vacated his seat weeks earlier for reasons of poor health, an unexpected move which impacted the lives of...nobody. ("Hey, the Pope retired. Pass the salt.")

Huddled behind closed doors, the 114 men of the Papal Conclave then cast secret ballots, counted the ballots, burned the ballots, cast some more ballots, counted the new ballots, burned the new ballots, and then repeated the process another dozen times, periodically pausing to argue over who might eventually get to be the Camerlengo that taps the next Pope on the forehead with a hammer.

As that little zinger is undoubtedly going to gnaw at you, I'll quickly explain.

The Camerlengo (Italian for "Chamberlain") of the Holy Roman Church is a high-ranking Cardinal charged to officially determine and announce that a reigning Pope is dead. Speculation abounds as to the Camerlengo's exact role, but there are reports (aka: rumors) of a ritual dating back to the Middle Ages where the Camerlengo taps the Pope's head with a silver hammer[22] and then calls out his baptismal name three times. The Church strongly denies[23] that any hammers are involved in the death ceremony, or that the calling out of the Pope's name is a requirement. John L. Allen's book "The Rise of Benedict XVI"[24] mentions no hammer, but Allen does refer to three *sprinkles* of holy water and the waving of incense over a Pope's lifeless body. It's very secretive, but all agree that the Camerlengo oversees some kind of ceremony, that three seems to be the agreeable number for whatever taps, sprinkles or waves are implemented, and the confirmed death of the reigning pontiff makes it obvious that a replacement Pope is in order. Firstly, though, the Vatican must spend approximately $847,859,748.33 on a televised papal funeral.

The case of Pope Benedict was unique in that he didn't vacate the throne through death, but instead simply abdicated. Regardless, with the absence of a supreme pontiff, the conclave chimney poured black

---

22 "Cardinal Camerlengo: Roman Catholicism". *Encyclopedia Britannica*. Encyclopedia Britannica, 2015. Web.

23 De la Garde Grissell, Hartwell. *Sede Vacante, being a Diary written during the Conclave of 1903, with additional Notes on the Accession and Coronation of Pius X*. Oxford and London: James Parker and Co. 1903. Page 2 and footnotes. Print.

24 Allen Jr., John L. *The Rise of Benedict XVI*. Doubleday Religion: New York. 2005. Pages 51-52. Print.

smoke into the sky, an ominous message to the overwrought masses that (gasp!) WE HAD NO POPE!

News cameras fixated upon the chimney and the dark cloud billowing out of it. International news agencies broadcast smoke status updates. Websites provided "smoke cams" with 24-hour live feeds. Indeed, the planet was obsessed with smoke, aching for the moment when its color would finally transition from black to white and allow 1.2 billion Roman Catholics to get back to their beers and bingo.

Upon his selection, Catholicism's new hero was required to rename himself, which makes perfect sense. ("We choose you. Now be somebody else.") And from smoke to saint, that's how Jorge Mario Bergoglio became Pope Francis, a near-deity hired to spend the rest of his days dodging the church's rampant sexual abuse scandals and attempting to sympathize with poor people by tossing cheery platitudes down from the throne of a church business worth hundreds of billions of dollars. (The Catholic Church's operating budget is $170 billion[25] in the U.S. alone.)

To the (literal) masses, this method for pontiff selection seems perfectly sensible, even routine. For the faithful, it's absolutely reasonable to cast secret ballots, blow smoke and huddle secretly while dressed up like 11th century chess pieces. This is their *normal*, and it's merely the appetizer in a feast of bizarre Catholic beliefs and practices. After all, this is the same church that asks its followers to pray to their deity's *mom*,[26] reflected in the common Catholic saying, "To Jesus, through Mary" (which sounds accidentally perverse). Apparently, as we funnel our requests to the blessed virgin, she acts as a lobbyist on

---

25   M.V., "The Catholic Church in America: The Working". *The Economist*. 16 August 2012. Web.

26   Catholic Tradition. "Why Catholics Pray to the Virgin Mary". *CatholicTradition.Org*. 2015. Web.

our behalf,[27] which implies that her omniscient son (who is also his own father) requires convincing. Mary is the female version of Tom Hagen from "The Godfather."

Of course, Mary's role becomes even more difficult to understand when you read the words of 1 Timothy 2:5, "For there is one God, and there is one mediator between God and men, the man Christ Jesus." I don't see Mary mentioned anywhere in that verse. Do you?

Mary's council could have saved us some time and angst regarding this whole Pope appointment thing, as his selection is such an important decision. Pope-hood transforms a mere mortal bishop into a kind of

---

27 United States Conference of Catholic Bishops. "Mary and the Saints". *USCCB.Org*. 2015. Web.

planetary *über*-priest, endowed with a special helping of God's power. In fact, the Roman Catholic Church holds to a concept called "Papal Infallibility," which declares that the Pope is infallible as long as three specific conditions are met:[28]

1.) He must be making a decree on matters of morality or faith.

2.) The declaration must be binding on the whole church.

3.) He must speak with the full authority of the Papacy, and not in a personal capacity.

Again, this seems rather curious to the observer. The Pope is the man. He's the Bishop of Rome. He's the pinnacle of spiritual authority and God's proxy here on earth. (The word "Pope" is actually rooted in the Latin word "papa," a child's word for "father.") And if you apply Merriam-Webster's definition of "infallible," the Pope has "the inability to be wrong." The concept of papal infallibility hearkens back to the biblical New Testament, specifically relating to Christ's promise to another of the appointed, Peter, declaring that he would be protected from error.[29]

The thing is, the Catholic Church has apparently decided that "infallible" is an on/off toggle switch hidden under Francis' frock. The Pope is infallible...except when he isn't, and to explain this concept to the thick and oblivious common folk, the church has produced pages and pages (and pages!) of apologetics material. The CatholicAnswers.com website[30] declares outright that "the Catholic Church's teaching on papal infallibility is one which is generally misunderstood by those outside

---

28   Catholic Online. "Theological Definition" (Papal Infallibility). *Catholic.Org*. 2015. Web.

29   Vatican City: Libreria Editrice Vaticana. *Catechism of the Catholic Church: Revised in Accordance with the Official Latin Text Promulgated by Pope John Paul II*. Sections 552-53. 1997. Web.

30   Catholic Answers. "Papal Infallibility". *Catholic.Com*. 2015. Web.

the Church. In particular, Fundamentalists and other 'Bible Christians' often confused the charism of papal 'infallibility' with 'impeccability.'"

AHAH! The pope is impeccable! (Definition: Not capable of sinning or liable to sin. Free from fault or blame. Flawless.)[31]

Except...when he isn't.

This is a tap dance that would put Fred Astaire to shame. Popes aren't perfect, but they can promote perfection. The Pope and Bishops can be infallible, er, impeccable, but neither of these terms necessarily indicate the absence of sin, which denotes fallibility. Individual church leaders don't enjoy the "prerogative of infallibility," but they can preach and proclaim Christ's infallible message, provided the message comes from God and isn't tainted by imperfect, human perceptions. The term "infallibility" applies to teachings put forth in "doctrinal unity," so the Pope and Bishops aren't necessarily infallible unless they've reached ecumenical agreement.

This comically nebulous lawyer-speak conveniently provides the Church an escape hatch whenever the Pope does something like, say, propose a Catholic open-door policy of welcome in regard to "homosexual persons" lending their gifts to ministry, as he did in the Vatican at the October 2014 Synod of Bishops assembly. That proposal caused the bishops serious consternation, as they seem to have actually read the Bible's decidedly "Fred Phelps" position on the subject of gays. The Holiest And Most Spiritually-Endowed Person On Planet Earth found himself at the wrong end of a majority vote (why, again, are we voting on God's will?), and all parties attempted to explain their private disagreements and divisions by publicly pontificating about unity.[32]

31 "Impeccable, adj." *Merriam Webster Online*. Encyclopedia Britannica, 2015. Web.
32 McKenna, Josephine. "Catholic bishops narrowly reject a wider welcome to gays, divorced Catholics". Religion News Service. 18 October 2014. Web.

The Pope also apparently received a garbled message from God on the subject of divorcees being allowed to take communion, as the bishops shot that proposal down like skeet in the very same meeting. (Hey, if the Supreme Pontiff can't get clarity on this stuff, perhaps God's throat could use a lozenge).

While we're speaking about relationships, can someone explain why a clerical celibate is giving sexually-active, consenting adults advice on horizontal refreshment? Shouldn't one criterion for relational counseling be that the advisor has studied the science of human sexuality and coupling beyond the Song of Solomon? And does anyone else see the irony, as homosexuals are discriminated against by fancily-dressed men who do not keep the company of women and disappear in secluded rooms for long periods of time?

Pope Francis shocked the world in that same month when he announced that "God is not a magician," and that Christians should embrace evolution and the Big Bang. Speaking to a plenary assembly of the Pontifical Academy of Sciences in October 2014, Francis said, "When we read about Creation in Genesis, we run the risk of imagining God was a magician, with a magic wand able to do everything - but that is not so."

At that moment, a host of high-ranking bishops immediately soiled themselves. History reveals the Vatican's slow dance around Darwin's "On the Origin of Species" after it published in 1859, at least until Pope John Paul II declared (only 137 years later) that there is "no conflict" between evolution and Catholicism.[33] And now a papal declaration that God isn't a magician able to do everything? Scandalous.

Perhaps an infallible, robed advisor should slip a note under Francis'

---

33   Pope John Paul II. "Message to the Pontifical Academy of Sciences: On Evolution." *Eternal Word Television Network*. 22 October 1996. Web.

door reminding him God/Jesus:

1.) created the universe from nothing (conjuring).

2.) turned rivers to blood (curses).

3.) transformed water to wine (tricks).

4.) walked on water (levitation and/or the ability to fly).

5.) grants wishes (the power to manipulate matter, space and time).

Seems pretty clear that Yahweh has been pulling rabbits out of his hat since the beginning of time. Yet despite his demonstrations of magical miracles on the universal stage, "God is not a magician," and somehow God's biblical book of Genesis jives with the natural processes of evolutionary biology. (I can't be too hard on the Pope for his confusion on issues related to God and science. After all, he belongs to the same church that condemned Galileo for his heretical claim that the sun didn't revolve around the earth. Science isn't exactly the Catholic Church's strong suit).

I suppose we can't talk about the office of the Pope without mentioning that gold mine of memes, gags, parodies and punchlines: the Popemobile.[34]

No, that isn't the vehicle's official name, but it's the only name ever given by anyone to the custom-fitted vehicles used by popes for public appearances in outdoor environments. In early days, the Pope was hoisted up on a chair and carried down the streets. Motor vehicles

---

34   Grünweg, Tom. "The Popemobile: A Brief History of the World's Holiest Car". *Spiegel Online International (Germany)*. 22 September 2011. Web.

were introduced in the 1930s, and after the May 1981 assassination attempt against Pope John Paul II, popemobiles have been outfitted like tanks, with thick armor plating and enclosures made of bullet-proof glass, bringing the vehicle weight to a gas-guzzling three metric tons. Popemobile manufacturers include A-team names like Mercedes, Cadillac and Ferrari, and don't try finding one of these puppies on Craigslist; the sticker price comes in just north of a half a million dollars. His holiness rides in style.[35]

Despite its blue chip pedigree and global fame, the Popemobile remains an awkward sight to behold. The vehicle looks like someone welded a carnival dunk tank onto the back of a pickup, and when camera angles obscure the lower vehicle behind thousands of spectators, the Popemobile makes the supreme pontiff look like a plastic-packaged action figure. (Years ago, I posted a Popemobile meme bearing the caption, "It's important to keep your Pope vacuum-sealed for maximum freshness.")

Does any adherent to the idea of divine protective power see the irony in having to encase God's Governor in a portable safe room? Shadrach, Meshach and Abednego walked a fiery furnace unsinged by flesh-consuming flames as Yahweh encased all three men in an impenetrable protective cloak, but a Pope's protection plan requires two inches of man-made bulletproof glass, heavy steel and a shit-ton of Swiss Guards? Curious behavior if one genuinely believes his deity could easily block an assassin's round with the flick of a divine fingernail. Perhaps God loses those precious seconds because he's being counseled on bullet trajectories by his mother.

In regard to Pope Francis the man, I'll admit that he seems friendly, accessible and refreshingly candid, the kind of guy who'll bust open

---

35   Day, Matthew. "Popemobile to Go Green" *The Telegraph (U.K.)*. June 2011. Web.

the communion wine bottles for a drink with friends when nobody is looking, and I can see why so many look with favor upon The People's Pope, this maverick who earned Time magazine's 2013 "Person of the Year" award.[36] Francis speaks in plain English. He exhibits compassion for the downtrodden and often walks the dirtiest of slums in his pristine papal robe. He stops for photos with his admirers and understands how to relate to a 21st century flock. He has demonstrated a long-overdue attitude of tolerance for non-heterosexuals and even atheists, asking "Who am I to judge?" And he nixed the Popemobile in favor of a used Renault with over 180,000 miles on the odometer, often driving *himself* around the Vatican![37]

For an infallible man enjoying stratospheric fame, Jorge Mario Bergoglio seems awfully down to earth.

But as much as I hate to pour cold water on everyone's communion wafer, it's important we not forget that Saint Frank remains the willing Master of Ceremonies for a church parade that once prevented its own flock from reading the Bible in English. That has a history of delightful gems like the Inquisition, witch hunts, book burnings and an alliance with those bastions of infallibility, the Nazis.[38] That has permanently posted a "No Girls Allowed" sign on its halls of power. That teaches (with a straight face) that condoms make the AIDS epidemic worse.[39] And that discriminates against good people who don't fit into the narrow cookie cutter of Catholic-approved sexuality. Add the fog of clandestine Vatican Bank activity, some large doses of corruption, and the

36   Chua-Eoan, Howard, and Dias, Elizabeth. "Pope Francis: The People's Pope".
     Time Magazine. 11 December 2013. Web.
37   Curry, Colleen. "Why Pope Francis Is Different From His Predecessors". *ABC News*. 11
     December 2013. Web.
38   Krieg, Robert A. *Catholic Theologians in Nazi Germany*. New York: Continuum. Page 6.
     2004. Print.
39   Squires, Nick. "Pope Benedict XVI: condoms make Aids crisis worse". *The Telegraph*
     (U.K.) 17 March 2009. Web.

centuries-old game of "Hide the Pedophile Priest,"[40] and the joy-joy feelings about Pope Francis' winning smile tend to fade a bit.

As the current Pope was born in 1936 (and I sincerely wish him a good, long life), it's inevitable that we will soon see the frothing and fawning begin again over the Pope selection process. Francis will receive the requisite three taps, waves or sprinkles, the media will focus its ratings-starved lens on the Papal Conclave chimney, and another costume ball will commence. A gaudy religious institution will again declare that it has a hotline to the mind of God, and it will announce His perfect will with big money, secret meetings and a billow of smoke.

Could the symbolism be any more profound?

---

40   Bruni, Frank. "Suffer the Children". *The New York Times*. 10 September 2012. Web.

O gentle cau,
Contented frau,
   Inert, exempt from violence.
We will allau
That you know hau
 To chew your cud in siolence.
"The Cow: a Bovinity"
  –Anonymous

CHAPTER 4
Sacred Cows

Being a native Oklahoman, I'm no stranger to the sight of cows. They graze along the fences. They're lined up in stalls at every state fair. A hilltop dairy facility along Interstate 44 has three fiberglass cows looming over the traffic as if they are counting cars. Oklahoma State University has the cowboy as its mascot.

If they had wings, I'd wager that cows would be our official state bird.

But a sacred animal? Not so much. Cows are rounded, herded, branded, and often served up between sesame seed buns. They're the cream for cheese and butter. They're oleo oil for margarine and shortening. They're the chucks, ribs, loins and shanks under glass at the meat counter. They're the suede shoes in the fall catalogs and the leather seats in luxury cars. They're the keratin in the extinguishing foam used by many fire and rescue teams.

You may not realize it, but it's possible that, at this very moment, you're surrounded by cows. After all, you can find bovine tallow in everything from wax paper to crayons to rubber to lipstick.[41] It's possible that the buttons on your shirt are made from cow bones. The strings on your

---

41   Agricultural Awareness Coalition of Nebraska. "Just the Facts… Beef Byproducts". *University of Nebraska*. Web. 2015.

tennis racket might be bovine intestines.[42] The cow might be the gelatin in your dessert, the wallet in your back pocket, the soap in your shower stall, the paint on your canvas (and even the bristles on your brush).[43]

In fact, American football fans might be surprised to learn that the "pigskin" footballs aren't actually made of pigs, but of cattle hides.[44] Still, I'd wager the whole of football fandom doesn't want to watch its favorite teams "throw the old cowskin."

In the eyes of many, cows are simply a resource born and bred to serve another purpose, and the idea of holding this lumbering beast of the field in high esteem seems ludicrous. To others, the treatment and execution of this docile animal to serve the marketplace is an unnecessary and cruel affront to all moral creatures. Take that perspective a few inches further, and you just might stumble upon the Hindu.

The planet's third largest religion, Hinduism is a melding of religion, culture, philosophy and tradition that defies a simple definition. Its name is taken from the Sanskrit, "Sindhu," the historical name of Northern India's Indus River, and it was a term used by foreigners to reference the people who lived around those waters. By the 16th century, India was often referred to as Hindustan (translated: the land of Hindus).[45]

As such, "Hindu" originally referred to a group of people, not a religious belief. In fact, the word "Hinduism" isn't found anywhere in The Rig Veda, one of the four canonical texts of Hindu scripture. The Vedas allegedly date as early as 6500 BCE, they're considered to be of divine

---

42   Mottershead, Clare. "The unusual uses for animal body parts". *BBC News (U.K.)*. 7 June 2011. Web.
43   Dairy Max. "Cattle By-Products". *DairyMax.Org*. 2015. Web.
44   See Footnote 41.
45   Thompson Platts, John. *A dictionary of Urdu, classical Hindī, and English*. W.H. Allen & Co., Oxford University. 1884. Web.

origin, and they're populated with a vast array of hymns, songs, formulas, chants, mantras and incantations in regard to a huge host of various gods and goddesses, the most fundamental being the Trimurti[46] of Brahma (the creator), Vishnu (the preserver) and Shiva (the destroyer).

The Hindus have deities like my wife has shoes, and a huge host of gods enjoys a place at the Hindu mythological table. There's Agni, the fire god. Mohini, the enchantress. Yama, lord of death. Chandra, god of the moon. Saraswati, the goddess of knowledge, music, art, wisdom and nature. Hanuman, the divine, shape-shifting monkey man. There's Parvati, the maternal form of Mother Goddess Gauri Jagadamba, who is also another incarnation of Shiva's wife, Shakti, who is also a form of the Great Goddess Durga and OH MY GOD, THIS STUFF IS INSANELY COMPLICATED!

46 Violatti, Cristian. "The Vedas: Definition". *Ancient History Encyclopedia*. 18 January 2013. Web.

    a. Hunter, Samantha. "Hinduism's God & Goddess Votives". *University of Missouri, Museum of Anthropology*. 2008. Web.

Delve into the deep, churning mythology of Hinduism for awhile, and you might want to rest your brain by learning Mandarin Chinese. The overlapping lists of gods and goddesses is the stuff of encyclopedias and far too vast and complex (and often contradictory) for these humble pages.

Suffice it to say that summarizing Hinduism ain't easy, especially for a guy who thinks Shiva sounds like a brand of car stereo, but the general gist is that we are all enduring souls that transmigrate from form to form, body to body, lifetime to lifetime, and our actions determine the form in which we will one day return to this world. In other words, what goes around…comes around.

Yes, we're talking about karma.

In Sanskrit, the word karma means "action and the consequences of action."[47] Intentional actions ripple outward to affect others, for good or for ill, and those actions will determine the form of your eventual reincarnation. It's like that internet meme which says, "Karma's a bitch, but only if you are," so it's a good idea to be kind, tell the truth, live an honorable life, and do whatever is necessary to ensure that you won't spend the precious short moments of your next life as a feeder rodent at the Reptile Emporium.

Hindus were once cow-eaters, but perhaps influenced by vegetarian Jainism (or the high expense of processing meat), they ultimately nixed beef from the menu and gave cows protected status. Contrary to popular belief, today's Hindus aren't necessarily vegetarians themselves, and some still enjoy a diet of meats and fishes.[48] Hindu dietary rules seem

---

47   Ellwood, Robert S. and Alles, Gregory D. *The Encyclopedia of World Religions*. Infobase Publishing. 2008. Web.
      a.   "Karma". *Encyclopedia Britannica*. Encyclopedia Britannica, 2015. Web.
48   Srivastava, Jane. "Vegetarianism and Meat-Eating in 8 Religions". *Hinduism Today Magazine, by Himalayan Academy*. April/May/June, 2007. Web.

to be as vast and varied as its deities, and contrary to public perception here in the United States, Hindus don't necessarily worship the cow (although cow products like milk and dung are integrated into worship rituals). However, the cow is revered as the source of food and the symbol of all life.[49] It hearkens back to the great Lord Krishna, said to be a cow herder 5,000 years ago. The cow is sacred. It provides a kind of role model. It is gentle and passive. It gives more than it takes. And outside of the 500 liters of daily methane erupting from its orifices, it's completely inoffensive.

The western concept of cow life in India is much more romantic than the reality of it. While they're pretty much guaranteed not to wind up as a leather jacket or a rump roast, the cows of India live a largely unglamorous existence. They meander about in public places and are ignored in the way that you and I might ignore a parked car. Many are neglected and malnourished, surviving on garbage and scraps on the street.[50] It's obvious that, even in Hindu country, being a cow ain't all that.

However, as every dog has his day, so does the cow, and on the 8th lunar day in the month of Karttika, the festival of Gopastami[51] ("cow day") honors all cows, cow lovers and caretakers. It's a celebration not only for all cows on earth, but also of Kamadhenu, the divine cow goddess referenced in scripture and known by the Hindu religion as the mother of all cattle. The backstory on Kamadhenu is spotty, but some believe that she functions as a kind of mother goddess, a mooing

---

49   "Holy Cow: Hinduism's Sacred Animal". *Public Broadcasting Service: Nature*. 4 June 2008. Web.
    a.   "Why do Hindus worship the cow?" *Hinduism Today Magazine, by Himalayan Academy*. April/May/June, 2004. Web.
50   Popham, Peter. "How India's sacred cows are beaten, abused and poisoned to make leather for high street shops". *The Independent (U.K.)*. 14 February 2000. Web.
51   "Celebrating Gopastami in Krishna Temples". *Festivals in India*. 2015. Web.
    a.   Risal, Ananta. "Gopastami- An auspicious day for cow celebration- Story 6". *Anantagopalrisal*. 17 June 2013. Web.

matriarch, all other deities living inside her body, with the four books of the Vedas represented by her legs. She also possesses the divine power to grant wishes to those she looks upon with favor. In fact, Kamadhenu translates, "wish cow." (And couldn't we all use one of those?)

There are bovine shrines, like the Bull Temple in Bangalore which honors the demigod, Nandi, servant of Shiva.[52] The ownership of cows is usually considered a sign of affluence or wealth. And if you're a Hindu wanting to impress that special someone with a present, the cow is considered to be the highest of all gifts,[53] although I'm not sure how that works out for those living in one-bedroom apartments.

---

52   "Bull Temple Bangalore". *Bangalore, the Garden City*. 2015. Web.
53   Das, Subhamoy. "Holy Cows: Hinduism's Blessed Bovines". *About Religion*. 2015. Web.

Of course, the cow isn't the only revered animal in Hinduism, and animal worship is common well outside of "Hindustan." Whales are considered a sacred icon and lucky charm in parts of Vietnam,[54] with villages often holding funeral services and ornate burials whenever they encounter a dead whale carcass on the beach. The Chinese honor the tiger -one of the twelve zodiac animals and a symbol of earth- with temples, dances, statues and art. Tigers also guard dead ancestors, promote fertility and are just seen as generally badass.[55] In Madagascar, the patron deity is the lizard.[56] Many citizens of Thailand believe that the spirits of the dead can take up residence in elephants,[57] and Buddhists are especially keen on the white elephant,[58] which they believe is a sacred symbol of fertility and wisdom.

Still, amid the holy snakes, rats, bears, monkeys, hawks and horses held in high spiritual esteem out there, my favorite sacred animal remains the cow. Yeah, it's not exactly a sexy beast, but it prefers to walk instead of charge, it doesn't spend the whole day sleeping, it's smart enough to go where the grass is greener, and perhaps most importantly, it never cries over spilled milk.

54   Bray, Adam. "Why Vietnamese villagers are dragging dead whales inland". *CNN Travel*. 25 February 2010. Web.
55   Guynup, Sharon. "Why Have Tigers Been Feared and Revered Throughout History?" *National Geographic*. 9 April 2014. Web.
56   "Ancient Religions". Encyclopedia Britannica. Ed. Hugh Chisolm. Page 52. 1910. Web. 2015.
57   DeMello, Margo. "Animals and Society". Columbia University Press. 2012. Print.
58   Choskyi, Jampa. "Symbolism of Animals in Buddhism". *Buddhist Himalaya*, Vol. 1 No. 1. 1988. Web.

CHAPTER 5
Are You Naked Under Those Clothes?

Some will accuse me of picking the low-hanging fruit on this one, but in my opinion, no book about bizarre beliefs and traditions should omit one of the most famous (yet rarely understood) religious customs: the wearing of Mormon Temple Garments.

The Mormon Church (The Church of Jesus Christ of Latter-Day Saints) is everywhere. In recent years, Mitt Romney, devout Mormon and 2012 U.S. Presidential candidate, hit the spotlight (providing late-night comedians with plenty of "magic underwear" punch lines), and he's just one name in a long list of famous LDS church members.

Fellow politician Harry Reid, one-time Senate majority leader, has said that his Democratic values mirror Mormon values.[59] Vampire romance novelist, Stephenie Meyer, author of the beloved "Twilight" series, has roots in the Latter Day Saints. Stephen R. Covey, author of the mega-selling book, "The 7 Habits of Highly Effective People," was once president of the Irish Mission of the Mormon church. Popular radio host Glenn Beck is an adherent of Mormonism. I grew up watching "Donnie & Marie," a variety show hosted by Mormon siblings Donnie

---

59   Walch, Tad. "Reid gets warm reception at BYU". *Deseret News*. 10 October 2007. Web.

and Marie Osmond, two fresh-faced, clean-cut poster children for family values who remain popular on television today. Aaron Eckhart, brilliant as "Two-Face" Harvey Dent in the Batman flick, "The Dark Night," graduated from Brigham Young University (owned by the LDS church). Andy Reid, head coach of the Kansas City Chiefs, is a Mormon. Hell, even the CEO of the Marriott hotel chain is a Mormon.[60]

So the rest of us have to wonder...are all of these people secretly wearing Almighty Tighty Whities?

Before we tackle a question of such gravity, we must first gain a better understanding of the LDS church, its origins, and elements of its basic doctrine. Some of this sounds a bit crazy, so I've ranked each item on a Batshit Scale of one (🦇) to four (🦇 🦇 🦇 🦇).

1) **The Mormon Church Sneezes Money and says "Bless you."**

Rating: 🦇

The Mormon church is ranked by the National Council of Churches as the fourth largest Christian denomination in the United States, boasting over 14 million members.[61] It operates in modest facilities, donates almost all of its revenues toward the care of the poor, sick and oppressed, spends all excess income on global efforts to find cures for cancer and AIDS, and...

GEEZ, I CRACK MYSELF UP!

---

60 "The List: Famous Mormons". *Washington Times*. 21 October 2011. Web.
61 "Facts and Statistics". *Mormon Newsroom: The Official Resource for News Media…* The Church of Jesus Christ of Latter-Day Saints. 2015. Web.

Actually, the LDS church is such a self-consciously gaudy mess that it makes Elvis Presley's Graceland estate look like a pup tent. It owns about $35 billion in temples worldwide and brings in an estimated $7 billion annually in tithes and donations.[62] (Remember Mitt Romney, who I mentioned at the beginning of this chapter? He singlehandedly gave over $4 million to the LDS church between 2010 and 2012.)[63] The Mormon church operates universities, newspapers, banks, restaurants, hotels, ranches, farms, parks, shopping malls and other businesses at huge profits.[64] Not bad for a religion that represents 2%[65] of the U.S. population.

The Mormons proclaim with pride that they don't have paid clergy, but there's a huge fog of mystery around labels like "unpaid" and "professional," and as the church provides inside banking services, the fee structures for leaders are anything but transparent. An organization called the Mormon Research Ministry apparently got its hands on a leaked copy of the 2006 Mission President's Handbook with guidelines regarding reimbursement for "necessary living expenses," and it estimated that a mission president's "unpaid" position might bring in over $100,000 annually.[66] Humble servants indeed.

And while we're chatting about money...

---

62   Henderson, Peter. "Mormon church earns $7 billion a year from tithing, analysis indicates". *NBC News*. 13 August 2012. Web.
63   IRS Filings for Mitt Romney, 2010 (page 140) and 2011 (page 69). Web.
64   Adwar, Corey. "These Magnificent Temples Point To How Rich The Mormon Church Is". *Business Insider.* 6 August 2014. Web.
65   "Religious Landscape Survey". *Pew Research: Religion and Public Life Project*. 2013. Web.
66   "Mormon Mission President's Handbook". *The Church of Jesus Christ of Latter-Day Saints*. Salt Lake City, Utah. 2006. Appendix B. Web.

2) **Joseph Smith was a Prophet for Profit**.

Rating:

Born in Sharon, Vermont in 1805, and founder of the LDS church, Joseph Smith grew up believing in things like prophecy and supernatural visions. In the 1820s, he advertised himself as a "seer," helping other people seek buried treasure (for a fee, of course). In fact, Smith was part of a treasure hunting company which often dodged charges of fakery from skeptics and unfulfilled clients, and Smith himself went to court for that reason in 1826. For obvious reasons, he moved around a lot.

3) **The Book of Mormon was Translated with a Magic Rock**.

Rating:

Actually, the story of the LDS holy book doesn't begin with a rock. It begins with a psychic, an angel and a book of golden plates. The tale is convoluted, so try and keep up.

Joseph Smith declared that, in 1823 at his parents' farm in Palmyra, New York, he had been visited by an angel. This angel led him to a buried book filled with golden plates, later described by "witnesses" as being comprised of thin gold pages, engraved on both sides, and bound with three rings, each plate weighing 30 to 60 pounds.

Smith wasn't allowed to take the plates. Instead, the angel instructed him to return the following year. Then the next year. And the next. Etc. (Tease!) Finally, in September of 1827, the angel brought to Smith those very plates which would ultimately become the Book of Mormon.

Oh, and did I mention that, in its original form, the language on the plates was reformed Egyptian, which wasn't exactly a second language in Palmyra, New York?

Fortunately, Joseph Smith, psychic seer and conduit of supernatural energy, was more than up to the task. No, he didn't understand reformed Egyptian, but he happened to be in possession of something he called a "seer stone," a chocolate-brown rock about the size of an egg. To gain benefit of the seer stone's powers, Smith had to place the rock in the bottom of a hat and then pull the hat over his face, the foreign text magically translating *through the stone itself*. (During the early translation, Smith described the use of seer stones set in a frame resembling a pair of large eyeglasses. He would see the translated text within the rock and simply dictate the translation to a scribe.) Once the translation was complete, Joseph Smith declared that he returned the gold plates to the angel.

So who originally engraved the reformed Egyptian onto the gold plates? According to the Book of Mormon itself, the text was written by two prophets and historians from around the year 400 CE, a father and son named Mormon and Moroni, Moroni ultimately being the angel that later appeared to Smith. (I told you it was complicated.) The returned and re-buried plates were never found, and many inside the Mormon faith believe they'll remain hidden until a future date of some significant, divine meaning.

Joseph Smith's translation of the golden plates was published on March 26, 1830 as the Book of Mormon, a holy text which contains all manner of divine revelation...including:

4) Ye Must Be Baptized...Even if You're Already Dead.

Rating:

The LDS church declares that baptism is absolutely necessary for salvation. 2 Nephi 31:11-12 states, "And the Father said: Repent ye, repent ye, and be baptized in the name of my Beloved Son." John 3:5 has Jesus declaring, "Except that a man be born of water and of the Spirit, he cannot enter the kingdom of God."

This becomes a challenge when one is immersed in dirt before he/she can be immersed in water.

I know what you're thinking. At this very moment, your mind's eye has conjured up some macabre scenario involving a backhoe and some smelling salts, but the Mormon ritual is actually rather benign, and it doesn't involve any actual corpses. In fact, the grateful dead remain asleep in their caskets as surrogates are selected to be dunked on their behalf. From the LDS church's own website:[67]

"People have occasionally wondered if the mortal remains of the deceased are somehow disturbed in this process; they are not. The person acting as a proxy uses only the name of the deceased. To prevent duplication, the Church keeps a record of the deceased persons who have been baptized. Some have misunderstood that when baptisms for the dead are performed, the names of deceased persons are being added to membership records of the Church. This is not the case."

And the practice isn't just for the faithful, as the LDS Church teaches that the unsaved still have the opportunity to accept the gospel of

---

67   "Baptisms for the Dead". *The Church of Jesus Christ of Latter-Day Saints.* 2015. Web.

Christ after death, providing that they receive all of the necessary or-
dinances (including baptism). There are also some wild references in
Mormon scripture about the actual location of God's kingdom, which
according to Joseph Smith's translation of an Egyptian scroll, is in
close proximity to a planet called Kolob.[68][69]

NOTE: If you're interested in a post-death resurrection, you might want
to strike cremation out of your Last Will & Testament, as it's a HELL of
a lot more difficult to restore your body from ashes in the afterlife.[70][71]

5) **Almost Everything is Forbidden.**

Rating:

In my work as an activist and radio host, I've had the opportunity
to interview ex-Mormons, and their descriptions of Mormon culture
sound suspiciously like...prison. Websites like lifeaftermormonism.net
and exmormon.org also paint the LDS Church as a kind of moral police state, where life's sweetest fruits are forbidden (or at the very least,
discouraged). Just a few examples:

- No R-rated films.
- No Sunday sports.
- No coffee or tea.
- No tobacco.
- Girls may have only their ears pierced, and only once per ear.
  (Boys are out of luck.)

68 *The Pearl of Great Price*: The Book of Abraham 3:1-4. The Church of Jesus Christ of Latter-
    Day Saints. 2015. Web.
69 "Translation and Historicity of the Book of Abraham". *The Church of Jesus Christ of Latter-
    Day Saints*. 2015. Web.
70 *The Book of Mormon*: Alma 40:23. The Church of Jesus Christ of Latter-Day Saints. 2015.
    Web.
71 Olsen, Bruce L. "Cremation". *Encyclopedia of Mormonism*. New York : Macmillan Publishing
    Company. 1992. Print.

- No tattoos.
- No masturbation (angels and your dead relatives are watching, folks).
- No role playing games, like "D&D" or "Magic: The Gathering."
- No alcoholic beverages.

On the upside, Mormons do get the privilege of paying 10% of their annual income to the LDS church for the whole of their adult lives.

6) **God is a Racist White Dude.**

Rating:

According to the Book of Mormon, a sect called the Lamanites (descendents of Laman and Lemuel, two Israelite brothers) split off from another group called the Nephites (founded by their righteous brother, Nephi),[72] and the two clans became the Hatfields and McCoys of pre-Columbus America. This is unfortunate, especially in light of the news that, only a few centuries before the fighting started, Jesus Christ himself stopped by for a post-resurrection "howdy" and converted both groups to Christianity.[73] [74]

Jesus visited America after the crucifixion. Just take a moment to digest that one.

The Lamanites eventually backslid into rebellion and sin, hating God and hating the Nephites, until God apparently flipped through his Retribution Rolodex for an appropriate punishment:

---

72 *The Book of Mormon*: 3 Nephi 11:18. The Church of Jesus Christ of Latter-Day Saints. 2015. Web.

73 *The Book of Mormon*: 3 Nephi 12:1-2. The Church of Jesus Christ of Latter-Day Saints. 2015. Web.

74 "Is it true that Jesus appeared in North America after his crucifixion and resurrection according to the Book of Mormon?". *The Church of Jesus Christ of Latter-Day Saints*. 2015. Web.

1) ~~Smite them with palsy.~~
2) ~~Execute their firstborn children.~~
3) ~~Bring on the locusts.~~
4) Turn them into black people!

2 Nephi 5:21-22

And he had caused the cursing to come upon them, yea, even a sore cursing, because of their iniquity.

For behold, they had hardened their hearts against him, that they had become like unto a flint; wherefore, as they were white, and exceedingly fair and delightsome, that they might not be enticing unto my people the Lord God did cause a skin of blackness to come upon them.

WTF?

And thus saith the Lord God: I will cause that they shall be loathsome unto thy people, save they shall repent of their iniquities.

(Perhaps the whole "skin of blackness" thing was the reason that the LDS church didn't allow blacks to enter the priesthood until 1978, a fact which has undoubtedly flushed the cheeks of many Mormon apologists. But for now, let's get back to the Lamanites and Nephites.)

The two tribes stood opposed, great battles ensued, and ultimately, the evil Lamanites wiped out the righteous Nephites and became commonly referred to within Mormon tradition as the ancestors of contemporary Native Americans.[75] Yes, Native Americans were declared the descendents of an evil people, at least until the church softened the language in its introduction to the Book of Mormon in 2004.[76]

Perhaps, one day, God will lift this plague of pigmentation upon blacks and Native Americans as he did for the Lamanites who repented in 3 Nephi 2:15,[77] "And their curse was taken from them, and their skin became white like unto the Nephites." And in the eyes of the Almighty, white...is right.

I could go on listing the offensive and bizarre elements of the Mormon church (polygamy, shunning, and Quakers living on the moon), but others have already covered LDS history and doctrine more effectively and in greater depth (like David Fitzgerald, author of "The Mormons," who slipped me fifty bucks for mentioning his book in this chapter).

Besides, I want to get back to the Mormon Temple Garments, those

75   Fletcher Stack, Peggy. "Single word change in Book of Mormon speaks volumes". *The Salt Lake Tribune.* 8 November 2007. Web.

76   Fletcher Stack, Peggy. "Church removes racial references in Book of Mormon headings". *The Salt Lake Tribune.* 20 December 2010. Web.

77   *The Book of Mormon*: 3 Nephi 2:15. The Church of Jesus Christ of Latter-Day Saints. 2015. Web.

precious (and protective?) pieces of underwear which are so revered by the LDS Church. What are they? And what do they do?

MTGs are worn by Mormon adults who have taken part in a ritual called the Endowment Ceremony, a secret (and seriously creepy) ritual where participants are symbolically washed and anointed, are consecrated to the LDS Church, and are provided symbolic names, passwords and hand gestures required by the angels who are guarding Heaven. The service is called an Endowment Ceremony, because participants allegedly receive an endowment - a gift - of heavenly power, as when Christ himself endowed the disciples with "power from on high" in Luke 24:49.

During this ceremony, participants receive the temple garments, symbolic reminders of the covenants made to God (and to the LDS Church) and sources of strength to resist evil and remain steadfast in the faith.

The Mormon Temple Garment comes in 1-piece and 2-piece varieties and has been modernized from an original 1840s version (which looks like your grandmother's lingerie). Modern MTGs have sleeves that stop midway to the elbow, leggings that stop just below the knee, and they bear several distinctive (and Masonic) symbols: On the left breast is the v-shaped **compass**, which represents an undeviating, straight course toward eternal life. On the right breast is the **square,** symbolizing the exactness, justice and fairness of God. At the navel sits a small **line**, representing strength and the constant need for nourishment in both body and spirit. And the right knee has a symbolic **split** in the stitching of the fabric, a reminder of the scriptural promise that "every knee shall bow" before God.[78] [79]

The temple garments encourage modesty, especially among women, as midriffs and miniskirts would look ridicuous with "bloomers" spilling beyond them. They come in standard white, although the LDS church has approved sand-colored garments for those who serve in the military. Also, military service personnel, police officers and firefighters can submit "regulation" t-shirts to have the symbolic markings added.[80]

For Mormons working dangerous professions, MTGs might seem like a *really* good idea, as there are plenty of claims that temple garments have protected people from knives, bullets, crash injuries and all manner of malady. Bill Marriot of Marriott hotels (mentioned earlier) did

---

78   Buerger, David John. *The Mysteries of Godliness: A History of Mormon Temple Worship* (2nd ed.) Salt Lake City: Signature Books. 2002. Print.

79   Mister Sister (pseudonym). "Holy Mormon Underwear". *Sister Wives Blog*. 26 July 2011. Web.

80   "Garment Guidelines for Military, Police, or Fire Fighters". *Beehive Clothing*. 2015. Web.

an April 7, 1996 "60 Minutes" interview, where he told Mike Wallace that the garments supernaturally kept his skin from burning during a boat fire. Joseph Smith himself was killed in a jailhouse mob shooting after removing his garments, while LDS Second Counselor Willard Richards (still adorned and protected) escaped with his life.

The LDS Church pooh-poohs many of these assertions, and it's easy to understand why. Nobody wants to tell a Mormon family that it lost a son in military combat because he air-dropped onto the Taliban wearing unbleached cotton instead of Kevlar. With the "It's a Symbol of our Covenant" angle, the church is also much less likely to wind up in court over charges of false advertising. Indeed...just as a wedding ring reminds you that you're married (as if this is actually necessary), MTGs remind endowed Mormons that they are spiritually married to God.[81]

For this reason, only endowed Mormons are allowed to purchase the garments. Online purchases require an LDS membership record number. The underwear is to be worn at all times (unless you're participating in an action for which the garment is impractical...like swimming, showering, sex, etc). And just as a good, upstanding servant of God wouldn't expose boxers, bras and briefs, Mormons are required to keep their MTGs concealed beneath their outer clothing. Their covenant to God is a personal promise and a personal blessing.

One final note. Mormon Temple Garments are just a small part of a wider product line available for sale on the spiffy LDS store website.[82] The Mormon Church sells baptismal suits, towels, pleated trousers, socks and children's clothing. Order your leather-bound, 4-book combo featuring the Standard Works (sacred Mormon scriptures). Pick up

---

81   "Lesson 5: Learning from the Lord through Symbols". *Endowed from on High: Temple Preparation Seminar Teacher's Manual.* Pages 21-25. The Church of Jesus Christ of Latter-Day Saints. 2013. Web.
82   http://store.lds.org

some Mormon Tabernacle Choir on CD, or perhaps an inspirational DVD on the church's history. Get monthly exhortation for your teenager with a subscription to New Era Magazine. Or how about some full-color Jesus art? The LDS store offers prints ranging in price from $40 to $281, and they're a great way to add a little holiness to your humble home. And of course, all of these wonderful items and more can be toted around in your handy LDS carry-all bag.

Interestingly, as the store is a church and the church is a store, the revenue stream for these purchases remains largely hidden from sight. The temple endowment ceremonies may be secret, but they've got nothing on the back rooms that contain the bank statements. Other types of non-profits are required by the IRS to disclose finances, donors and personnel (Form 990), but the Mormon Church (and churches in general) simply wave the religion flag and enjoy automatic tax-exempt status.

If that doesn't get your underwear in a wad, nothing will.

CHAPTER 6
Death Becomes You

"…if you encounter things that shock or offend you, don't complain to us, **because you have been warned**."

Designed to both repel and tantalize, this ominous warning sits at the top of the website of the Church of Euthanasia.[83]

Euthanasia, of course, refers to the practice of intentionally ending a life as a way to relieve suffering. If you're afflicted with a terminal illness or live your life in agonizing pain, you can opt to punch your own ticket (or someone else's, if they're similarly afflicted) in a variety of controversial and often illegal ways. The practice is sometimes referred to as assisted suicide, physician-assisted suicide, and mercy killing. The late Dr. Jack Kevorkian, an American pathologist, gained worldwide fame by helping terminal patients (130, by his own account) end their own lives. The practice is currently banned in the USA in every state except Washington, Oregon, Montana, and Vermont, and it remains a highly polarizing issue across the planet.

Enter the Church of Euthanasia, an online political organization that encourages humankind to pursue voluntary population reduction. Its slogan: "Save the Planet, Kill Yourself."

---

83   www.churchofeuthanasia.org

At first glance, it's obvious that the Church of Euthanasia isn't much more than a handful of hipsters with a remarkably shitty website (it does boast "hundreds of card-carrying members"), but it has a genuinely intriguing doctrine, and in all honestly, it's not the first religion obsessed with the "big sleep.".

Founded by a techno musician and software developer in Boston, the Church of Euthanasia's website declares it a "non-profit educational foundation devoted to restoring balance between humans and the remaining species on earth." The CoE has one commandment: "Thou shalt not procreate."

Apparently, the overpopulation of humans is preventing a "compassionate, sustainable future." We breed too much. We eat too much. We take up too much space and oxygen. We've metastasized like a cancer. And we must be stopped.

I'm reminded of Agent Smith's speech to Morpheus in "The Matrix:"

"I'd like to share a revelation that I've had during my time here. It came to me when I tried to classify your species, and I realized that you're not actually mammals. Every mammal on this planet instinctively develops a natural equilibrium with the surrounding environment, but you humans do not. You move to an area and you multiply and multiply until every natural resource is consumed, and the only way you can survive is to spread to another area. There is another organism on this planet that follows the same pattern. Do you know what it is? A virus. Human beings are a disease, a cancer of this planet. You're a plague and we are the cure."

What's the cure? Well, the Church of Euthanasia asks its members to take a lifetime vow never to procreate (and while you're declaring your vow, don't forget to give the CoE that tax-deductible donation). In fact, suicide, while not discouraged, plays second fiddle to the birth control theme, with the CoE site going so far as to list resources for emergency contraception.

It all rather sounds like a frat party stunt, but the church's principals (called "pillars") do give one pause: suicide, abortion, cannibalism (yes, cannibalism) and sodomy. Each is a tool in the arsenal against overpopulation, a middle finger to the puritan religious, and a handy method for thinning the herd. They're also loaded terms guaranteed to generate publicity and get attention. (Who knows? They might even get mentioned in somebody's book!)

Of course, suicide, abortion, cannibalism and sodomy are serious, real-world issues, and with so many serious-as-a-heart-attack zealots in the blogosphere these days, I initially found it difficult to decide if I was reading the manifesto of an extremist or the provocative, shock-jock ramblings of a Poe.

Poe's Law: named after its author Nathan Poe, is an internet adage reflecting the idea that without a clear indication of the author's intent, it is difficult or impossible to tell the difference between an expression of sincere extremism and a parody of extremism.

The page on abortion contained Shakespearean wailings about witch-hunts against the "holy abortionist." Sodomy was pitched as a healthy way to prevent those pesky egg/sperm introductions. Readers were educated on the best way to consume their own pee ("the morning urine is the richest and best urine to drink"). When I browsed to the Cannibalism section about how the human "animal is neither built nor bred for its meat, and as such will not provide nearly as much flesh as a pig or cow," I immediately detoured into a macabre inner monologue about the logistics of eating a person. Would I? Could I? What if I faced starvation in the direst of circumstances? What if I had known them personally? Which portion would be the least repulsive to eat? Raw or cooked? Seasoned or unseasoned? Skin or skinless? Would they taste like jerky if they'd been a smoker?

And then it struck me. This is what the Church of Euthanasia wanted! It had dangled the (rather fleshy) bait in front of me and watched with glee as I chomped down, earnestly scrolling full paragraphs of straight-faced "doctrine" to suddenly discover a recipe for *Bob Arson's White Devil Dinky-Dao Mothafucka Bobbacoo Sauce*. (To its credit, it does include 2 tablespoons of whiskey.)

If all of this seems rather "supermarket tabloid," you won't be surprised to know that members of the Church of Euthanasia actually appeared on Jerry Springer's daytime talk show on the August 11th, 1997 episode titled, "I Want to Join a Suicide Cult." (Other groundbreaking Springer episodes that season included "I'm Pregnant by a Transsexual," "I Worked as a Sideshow Freak" and "I Refuse to Wear Clothes.")[84]

The Church of Euthanasia largely targets the most sensitive nerves of the Christian Right, reveling in its mission to heckle, irritate and inflame, and as its founder is still alive, it doesn't exactly reek of conviction. (At least Marshall Applewhite led his "Heaven's Gate" flock to the spaceship instead of merely tossing them a website link.) There's little doubt that that CoE does get people talking, and on the Batshit Scale, it still sits well below many of the other examples I've highlighted within these pages.

Perhaps most importantly, the Church of Euthanasia hasn't knocked on my door with pamphlets at nine o'clock on a Saturday morning, and that's the only "big sleep" I'm really interested in.

---

84   http://www.oocities.org/entertalkmentsite/jerryspringer.html

CHAPTER 7
Die in the Sky

Sometimes, in casual conversation with family members or friends (especially after reading chapters like my previous one), the topic will drift toward the themes of life and death. We'll wax on about how long we'd like to live (I'll take 86 years, thanks) and exactly how we'd like to check out (peacefully in my sleep, thanks). We'll share our bucket lists

of things we hope to accomplish before the inevitable dirt bath. And we'll almost always wind up discussing our own funerals: location of service, open-casket or sealed urn, burial attire, who gives the eulogy, which relatives will be barred at the door, and whether the exit song should be "Freebird" or "Dust in the Wind."

Here in the United States, funerals are almost always reserved and rather benign affairs. There's the preparation of the body, which takes place privately, far from the eyes of family and friends. There's a viewing, where people quietly hover and whisper that the mortician's makeup job somehow made Aunt Sadie look like Jack Palance. The ceremony itself is almost always a short church service, the rows of pews filled with a mixture of grieving loved ones and mildly sad casual acquaintances. Graveside services see the lowering of a casket into the ground, and then the crowd goes home for quiet contemplation and a cheese plate.

This is the typical funeral in contemporary America. But world history reveals that humankind has always had a wide palette of approaches to death, many of them strange and a few quite distressing.

Tenth century Scandinavian Vikings marked the death of a chieftain by burying him for ten days before digging him up and tossing him onto a wooden ship (next to a recently gang-raped and executed slave girl) to be set aflame…facilitating his voyage to the Realm of the Dead.[85]

The Dani people of West Papua, New Guinea recently practiced a bizarre (and now banned) funerary ritual, which required that the dead person's children and all closely-related females amputate one of their own fingers.[86] [87] The tradition was called "ikipalin," an outward representation of internal grief and suffering, and a sacrifice to appease the spirits. (The Dani also practiced cannibalism, which means each funeral amputation *must* have provided a fresh opportunity to say, "Hey… are you gonna eat that?")

---

85 Montgomery, James E. "Ibn Fadlan and the Risala". *Journal of Arabic and Islamic Studies*. Vol. 3. 2000. Pgs 12-19. Web.

86 Leo, P.J. "'Ikipalin' the finger-cutting tradition". *The Jakarta Post*. 15 September 2012. Web.

87 Favazza, Armando R. *Bodies Under Siege: Self-mutilation and Body Modification in Culture and Psychiatry*. Baltimore, Maryland: John Hopkins University Press. 1996. Pgs. 132-33. Print.

Another banned funeral tradition, called "Sati," was practiced in several Asian communities and dates back to the 4th century BCE. Essentially, a dead husband's body was ignited on a funeral pyre, and as she apparently forgot the whole, "till death do us part" portion of her vows, the recently-widowed wife would leap onto the burning pile and immolate herself.

In Southwest China's Gongzian County, the Bo people hung coffins from the sides of cliffs,[88] an act which was allegedly said to bless the eternal soul (and prevent animals from eating the remains).

In New Orleans, Louisiana, the "jazz funeral" is both a somber memorial and a raucous shindig, meshing African-American, West African and French tradition, as mourners are led by a marching band. The occasion begins slow and somber, but once the body is buried, jubilant music and dancing begin, and the affair becomes a celebration and commemoration: a mini Mardi Gras for the dearly departed.[89]

South Korea's scarcity of graveyard space spawned a law (passed in 2000) requiring loved ones to exhume the bodies of relatives after 60 years. But instead of simply cremating the uninterred remains, some families have started a tradition of having the bodies compressed into shiny "death beads," which are then kept in dishes and glass containers.[90] (Imagine a small terrarium filled with marbles. Now imagine that those marbles…are grandma.)

---

88   Liu, Tao Tao, and Faure, David. *Unity and Diversity: Local Cultures and Identities in China*. Hong Kong University Press, 1996. Print.

89   "The Jazz Funeral". Originally published in *The Soul of New Orleans*. Accessed via New Orleans Official Guide. 2015. Web.

90   "Turning the dead into beads: South Korea's 'odd' new trend". *The Week*. 24 January 2012. Web.
      a.   Kim, Hyung-Jin. "Ashes to beads: South Koreans try new way to mourn" *Associated Press*. 14 November 2011.

In parts of northern Japan, a few dozen Buddhist monks decided they wished to be mummified upon death and apparently wanted to do the honors of preparation themselves.[91] In a now-illegal ritual called "Sokushinbutsu," with roots dating back a millennium to the temples of Mount Koya, these monks ate nothing but nuts and seeds for three full years. While on this protein-crazy diet, they exercised rigorously to burn off the body's fat stores. After that, it was another 1,000 days of dining on tree roots before performing the coup de grace, the drinking of the poisonous sap of a Urushi tree while seated in a sealed stone tomb. Cue violent emissions of fluid from almost every orifice and a shutdown of the body's organs, and you had a band of self-mummified dead guys whose corpses were so toxic that even the maggots wanted nothing to do with them.

In Venezuela and Brazil, the Yanomami people believe that many deaths occur because demons are on the hunt for corpses to possess. Obviously, the idea of reanimated corpses driven by hell-spawn is a bit disconcerting, so the villagers quickly burn lifeless bodies, storing the ashes for a year before ultimately using them like you and I might use a bouillon cube. The dusty deceased are mixed into a big bowl of plantain soup, and this process (called "endocannibalism") is said to help the spirits of the dead continue down through the generations.[92]

Zoroastrians begin each funeral by cleaning the corpse with bull urine before the ritual of "Sagdid," which involves bringing in a dog that can cast out evil spirits.[93] The body is ultimately placed on the Tower of Silence, a cylindrical structure (also called a "Dakhmeh") surrounding a central pit. The bodies of the dead are placed on top of the tower

91   Aaron Lowe. "Shingon Priests and Self-Mummification". *Agora Journal*. 2005. Web.
92   Conklin, Beth A. *Consuming Grief: Compassionate Cannibalism in an Amazonian Society*. Austin, TX: University of Texas Press. 2001. Print.
93   Boyce, Mary. *Zoroastrians: Their Religious Beliefs and Practices*. London: Routledge. 1979. Print.

to bleach and rot in the sun as scavenging birds peck away at them. After more than a year, the remaining bones are swept into the pit and eventually disintegrate into the ground and sea. Ashes to ashes. Dust to dust.

The Zoroastrian process has many similarities with the Tibetan practice of "sky burial," which is also seen in other Chinese provinces like Qinghai, Sichuan and Mongolia and climaxes with a tall perch and a flock of hungry vultures. Known locally as "bya gtor" (which translates "alms for the birds"), sky burial adheres to Vajrayana Buddhism, which claims that consciousness can transmigrate, constantly being reborn in any number of forms, and once a consciousness is finished with a current form or shell, there's no reason to preserve the remains. Essentially, abandoning your old body is like leaving your rusted-out, 1978 Ford Pinto at the salvage yard after you pick up a new Mustang.

Sky burial[94] has its roots in ancient tradition, but it's also seen as a practical option for disposing of corpses. As Tibet's terrain is much too rocky and dense for traditional gravesites, and with wood for coffins and fuel for cremation in short supply, sky burial offers the dead as food to sustain living creatures. The prepared body is simply placed upon a high rock, and the carnivores come a'runnin.

Honestly, the tradition of sky burial doesn't seem that peculiar to me. Whether we're lowered into a hole or perched upon a mountain, the process of decay and decomposition remains the same. The atoms of our bodies are rearranged into the earth (and ultimately, the universe), and while I don't personally believe in a supernatural afterlife, I do see

---

94   Dorje, Gyurme, et.al. *The Tibetan Book of the Dead*: First Complete Translation. Penguin Classics Deluxe Edition. 2007. Print.
    a.   Mayhew, Bradley, et. al. *Tibet (Lonely Planet Country Guide)*. 7th ed. Australia: Lonely Planet. 2008. Page 48. Print.

that process as a kind of continued existence. In light of that, Tibetan sky burial is actually rather poetic.

But the advance preparation of the body *does* give me pause. The process is called "Jhator," and it begins on the third day of decomposition. The cadaver is cleaned and wrapped in a white cloth, juniper incense is burned and a monk chants the sacred mantra. Then…the rogyapas take over. Rogyapa translates, "body breaker," and believe me, that's exactly what these guys do. A senior-ranking rogyapa hacks the corpse into pieces, and then the whole troupe uses large rocks to smash the shit out of it. The remaining pulp is mixed with flour and yak butter, dragged to the sky burial site, and dinner is served.[95]

Poetic, my ass.

Look. I realize that the electrical impulses in my brain will cease at the

---

95 Mayhew, Bradley, et. al. *Tibet (Lonely Planet Country Guide)*. 7th ed. Australia: Lonely Planet. 2008. Page 48. Print.

moment of my death. When the heart stops ka-thumping, the lungs stop heaving, and the machine of my body grinds to a halt, I won't have a care (or the ability to care) about what's done with that cold, motionless lump on the slab that used to be me. But in advance of my death, I do have a measure of control over how I am memorialized, and if my death happens within 100 klicks of Tibet, I'm pretty certain I don't want to be remembered as the guy who got tied up in a sheet, dragged up a mountain and stomped into a meat pie.

No, you can give me the pomp, the mourners, the sad songs and the headstone. Sure, I might have traded vultures for worms, but the dark decay of my earthen sleep will be hid from sight, and for those that I leave behind, my passing might yet bring to mind that classic funeral ballad:

I'd like the memory of me to be a happy one.
I'd like to leave an afterglow of smiles when life is done.
I'd like to leave an echo whispering softly down the ways.
Of happy times and laughing times and bright and sunny days.
I'd like the tears of those who grieve to dry before the sun.
Of happy memories that I leave when life is done.

-Author unknown

CHAPTER 8
The Fortune Tellers

Before my office relocated to another part of the city, my morning commute used to take me by this tiny, turquoise house with a white door, chipped shingles, neglected lawn, cracked sidewalk and a neon sign in the window that said, "Palm Reading."

In the 21st century -the era of space flight and the decoded human genome- someone was selling the secrets to Life, the Universe and Everything from a rickety shack in the business district of Broken Arrow, Oklahoma. Go figure.

Of course, it's a long-running gag in the skeptic community that the vast, vast majority of these mediums and magicians operate out of houses, trailer parks and even tents, because they can't prognosticate a single winning lottery number. They predict our prosperity or doom, but they can't pick a winning stock. Or locate that hidden, priceless painting at an estate sale. Or hitch their wagon onto a soon-to-be-successful class action lawsuit. Or locate precious metals hidden beneath our feet. Or purchase the World Series seat where the home run ball will fall directly into their hands (and then onto a lucrative Ebay auction). Or purchase toy action figures that will one day become five-figure collectibles. Or secure cheap land before the announcement of a future shopping mall. Or walk up to the "Leprechaun's Gold" slot machine at the moment of the winning pull.

The vast majority of these people have somehow missed out on the "fortune" in fortune teller, instead peddling their divinations for whatever fee the market will bear.

Some (like me) see the very existence of a poor psychic as self-refuting. The argument that they cannot use their gifts for personal gain doesn't wash, as personal gain would actually allow them greater resources to bring greater gain to the rest of us. Instead of doing half-a-dozen, weekly psychic readings over a chipped, Formica desktop, they could operate from a self-financed Sears Tower of Soothsaying, exploring and explaining the love, laugh and life-lines of the global population.

There are wealthy psychics like millionaires John Edward and the late Sylvia Browne, but as they made their fortunes through book sales, honorariums, fees and traveling road shows, it can still be said that neither built their enterprises on the divined discovery of another Hope Diamond. Their prosperity was supply/demand, not supernatural. They simply sold tickets, and thousands happily paid.

And psychic work is actually pitched as a "get rich" scheme on many fronts. The website magiciansmakingmoney.com provides a home study course titled, "How Magicians Can Make Over $200 Per Hour as a Strolling Psychic Entertainer." The program provides tutorials on divination and fortune telling, with volumes on everything from Chinese numerology to tarot card readings to palmistry (and the entire program will only set you back $299.95).

Professed six-figure psychic Joe Nicols has published the book, "How to Make a Good Living as a Professional Psychic,"[96] which promises

---

96 Nicols, Joe. *How To Make A Good Living As A Professional Psychic.* West Yorkshire, U.K.: Tranquility Press. 1998. Print.

to "benefit the business practices of a wide range of metaphysical and holistic professionals, including massage therapists, healers and energy workers." His Amazon page actually promises tips for "using psychic techniques to manifest money." As the book is currently ranked #1,232,066 on Amazon Best Sellers, I suspect his personal manifestation of money hasn't come from author royalties.

Call me naive, but I'm amazed that the public hasn't cried out for a kind of Pay-Per-Hit business model, where the psychic's fee is only activated after a successful prediction. Such a scenario would protect the consumer from the fakes and fraudsters, and the price points could skyrocket, rewarding every "hit" with an instant and automatic payment. A risk-free prediction could name its own price. Everybody would go home a winner.

Unless, of course, the psychic gets it wrong. And as this happens so often in the psychic business, I'm genuinely surprised there haven't been riots.

Let's get back to Sylvia Browne. A famous celebrity psychic and spiritual medium, she was a regular feature on television shows like The Montel Williams Show and Larry King Live. In 2006, Browne even appeared as herself in the daytime soap opera, "The Young and the Restless."[97] She began her career as a psychic in 1974 and gained international fame. She published 45 books (best title: "All Pets Go To Heaven"). Browne often spoke of God (a deity comprised of both a male and female portion named Om and Azna, respectively). She prognosticated from the stage, the screen, and even via telephone, where (according to Browne's own website price list) she had charged up to $850 for a thirty-minute call session.[98] By 2010, the Sylvia Browne Corporation and Sylvia Browne Enterprises were pulling in a cool $3 million annually. Big business.

The problem is, Sylvia Browne couldn't find water if she fell off of the Titanic.

Thanks to resources like LexisNexis and exposés by organizations like the James Randi Educational Foundation and the Center for Inquiry, we have clear documentation of Browne's predictions and track record, and at the outset, we can see that it would have been better (and cheaper) to scrawl predictions onto a wall and hire a dart-throwing chimpanzee.

In 2010, Skeptical Inquirer published a lengthy analysis of Sylvia Browne's years of predictions specifically related to crimes, murder cases, and missing persons. It examined her claims from television shows (like Montel Williams, on which she was a regular), older predictions from newspaper articles, and the information she professed was divined from the spirit realm, to see how dialed-in her clairvoyant

97   Adams, Diane. "Young and the Restless Recap: December 18, 2006". Web.
98   "Sylvia Browne". *Official Website*. 2008. Web.

abilities were in regard to these human tragedies. Out of the 115 recorded predictions analyzed by S.I., her success rate came in at...zero.[99]

It gets better. Browne was a frequent consultant for (wait for it) *law enforcement agencies*, allegedly charging police departments up to $400 for her psychic services.[100] Her most famous failure is perhaps the 2003 criminal kidnapping case of Amanda Berry, a 16-year-old girl who was abducted on her way home from work. The following year, Amanda's mother Louwana joined Sylvia Browne on the Montel Williams show, desperate for news of her daughter's fate, and Browne delivered the worst possible news:[101]

"She's not alive, honey. Your daughter's not the kind who wouldn't call."

A full decade later, Amanda Berry was found alive, along with two other captives at a house in Cleveland, Ohio. But Amanda's mother was not there for the jubilant rescue and reunion. Louwana died in 2006, and to her dying breath, she was tortured with the belief that her daughter had been murdered.

Hell, Sylvia Browne even screwed up the prediction of her own death (at 88), falling short of that mark by eleven years![102]

Of course, her story is the rule, not the exception. Millions watched the humiliation of self-professed psychic and mentalist Uri Geller by James Randi on national television in 1973 during Johnny Carson's "Tonight Show." (It was beautiful.) Geller's claim to fame was the

---

99   Randi, James. "Yet Another Sylvia Browne Fiasco". *James Randi Educational Foundation, Swift Blog*. 7 May 2013. Web.
100   Shaffer, Ryan and Jadwiszczok, Agatha. "Psychic Defective: Sylvia Browne's History of Failure". *Skeptical Inquirer.* Vol 34.2. 2010. Web.
101   Curry, Colleen. "Psychic Who Said Amanda Berry Was Dead Silent After Berry Is Found Alive". *ABC News*. 7 May 2013. Web.
102   Owoseje, Toyin. "Psychic Sylvia Browne Falls Short of Own Death Prediction by 11 Years". *International Business Times*. 21 November 2013. Web.

ability to bend spoons *with his mind*, but when Carson swapped out the mentalist's spoons with separate ones, Geller's powers of psychokinesis dried up, and he suddenly declared that he did not "feel strong." A master mystifier had been trumped by a tray of kitchen utensils.

Of course, any illusionist can tell you that the spoon-bending stunt is the equivalent of "Who's got your nose?," a cheap trick any 10-year-old can pull off with just a few minutes of preparation (hint: you pre-bend the spoons repeatedly to soften them up). And this kind of nonsense would be harmless enough, except that Uri Geller apparently claims fat paychecks for his "abilities" as a psychic geologist (dowsing for oil or underground treasures), and a report by the BBC alleges that Geller was a paid psychic operative for the CIA during the Cold War,[103] purportedly exploring ways to dupe the KGB by (literally) blowing its mind.

If this is true, P.T. Barnum would be proud.

Psychic prediction, of course, is nothing new, and neither is its failure. Recently, prophesiers of doom predicted the end of the world in 2012, allegedly foreseen by the Mayans. LaMont Hamilton of WorldPsychic. org predicted that Prince William and Kate would have a baby girl.[104] Toronto, Ontario's "Psychic to the Stars" Nikki (she doesn't use a last name) warned that New York's Empire State Building would see a nuclear terrorist attack in 2013.[105] That same year, Los Angeles psychic celebrity Judy Hevenly wrongly predicted that new England Patriots quarterback, Tim Tebow, would get an offer to play for the Canadian Football League,[106] and Maine-based psychic Vicki Monroe mistakenly declared

103 Rees, Jasper. "Was Uri Geller hired as a spy by intelligence agencies?". *The Telegraph, U.K.* 21 July 2013. Web.

104 "Predictions - 2013 Part 1". *World Psychic- LaMont Hamilton.* 17 December 2012. Web.

105 Jones, Martha. "Psychic Nikki offers up her 2013 Predictions". *Examiner.com.* 29 December 2012. Web.

106 Nolan, Michel. "2013 predictions from a psychic". *Daily Bulletin.* 27 December 2012. Web.

that, in the wake of his divorce, Tom Cruise would finally leave the Church of Scientology.[107]

And then you've got psychics like Blair Robertson who are clever enough to keep things vague, as he predicted the 2013 deaths of "a number of former world heads of state as well as their spouses." With 196 countries providing heads of state and spouses (almost 400 people, many elderly), the percentages were already high that we'd see a few state funerals. Not exactly groundbreaking stuff.[108]

107 Wagner, Stephen. "Psychic Predictions for 2013". *About Entertainment*. 2012. Web.
108 Robertson, Blair. "2013 Psychic Predictions". *PRNewswire via Comtex*. 28 December 2012. Web.

One of my favorite "psychic" stories comes out of Japan. Yanagi Ryuken claimed to be an expert in the art of Kiai (psychic fighting), a skill which allegedly allowed him to kick your ass *without ever touching you*!

In martial arts, Kiai is actually a yell shouted before, during or after a certain technique, said to be an expression or projection of one's own internal energies. There are many variations on the definition of Kiai, but Ryuken (his last name translates "dragon fist") apparently defined it to include a melding of psychic intuition and psychokinesis, his powers brushing opponents away without any physical contact. In fact, YouTube videos of Ryuken show him effortlessly knocking his martial arts students to the floor. Amazing stuff.

Even more amazing was the $5000 wager which Ryuken offered to anyone who could overcome the power of his touchless takedowns…an offer so tasty, it was accepted by a genuine MMA fighter, Iwakura Goh, who proceeded to pound poor Yanagi like he was being tenderized.[109]

There are a great many techniques for prognostication in relation to the human body. Foot reading (also known as Solestry) is a holistic method for revealing emotions and personality, with your foot size, foot shape, "zones," toe gaps, toenails, toe webbing, bunions and calluses providing keen insights into your disposition, relationships, personality, past, present and future. Also important are your foot temperature and the condition of the chakras (which are explained in the chapter, "Rise Up and Walk"). Of course, there are organized learning programs on these techniques which will only cost you a weekend and a few hundred clams.

Moleosophy asserts that the placement, size and color of moles on your

---

109 Jenness, Kirik. "No touch martial arts master meets reality". *Underground Mixed Martial Arts*. 18 February 2013. Web.

body are windows into your character and destiny. By the definition of some, a mole found on the right side of your head predisposes you to politics. A mole on the ear predicts money and luxury. Nose moles betray a sharp temper. A mole on the left stomach denotes jealousy and laziness. And if you have a mole on your ass, you're likely to become an artist. Guidelines like these are allegedly derived from Indian and Chinese astrology and also have roots in early Greek culture. Strangely, mole predictions from different molesophers often directly contradict each other. Of course, as I have a mole on my neck, I'm said to be easily fooled, so perhaps I'm missing something.

The practice of Uromancy unlocks the psychic secrets of tomorrow by having you pee in a jar so that the urine can be examined for "omens." Trained pee-seers follow a urethra roadmap toward enlightenment via the observation of urine color, flow, spatter patterns, bubbles and (you knew this was coming) taste. For the morbidly curious, Occultopedia states that large bubbles spaced apart indicate positive health and wealth. Tiny bubbles clustered closely foresee illness, loss and even death. Regarding the taste thing, you're on your own.

We can't address psychics without mentioning the horoscope, a "fortune cookie" brand of prognosticating, where every vague message somehow sounds specifically targeted to one's own unique situation.

- Today will present a number of surprises which will keep you on your toes.
- You will gain an aura of quiet wisdom, the organic flow guiding your choices.
- Your astrological sign is positioned beneficially for love and happiness. But you must act quickly.
- Today looks to be a day of revelation as you feel a stronger sense of alignment from within and without.

- The needs of the many outweigh the needs of the few. Or the one. (Wait. That's from Trek. Never mind.)

Of course, these predictions are divided into the twelve signs of the zodiac:

ARIES: March 21-April 19
TAURUS: April 20-May 20
GEMINI: May 21-June 20
CANCER: June 21-July 22
LEO: July 23-August 22
VIRGO: August 23-September 22
LIBRA: September 23-October 22
SCORPIO: October 23-November 21
SAGITTARIUS: November 22-December 21
CAPRICORN: December 22-Jaunary 19
AQUARIUS: January 20-February 18
PISCES: February 19-March 20

My birthday is April 12th. I'm an Aries. According to Astrology.com's description of the Aries, my symbol is the ram. I am a natural leader, but I often lack long-term focus. I'm usually first in line to instigate something. I prefer to initiate a task rather than complete it. I have a personal magnetism. I'm impulsive. I'm blunt and to the point. I'm a pioneer, unafraid of breaking fresh ground. I'm loaded with energy and dynamism. And every day brings me pure bliss.

Apparently, the Aries is ruled by Mars, the god of war, and as a result, I have a predilection for confrontation. (But I still have daily bliss?) I can be construed as being arrogant. The color of the ram is bright red. My element is fire.

I originally read the above description and was struck by how much of the information rang true. I'm a leader (or at least a doer). I'm blunt and to the point. I'm not scared of change, and I'm occasionally known for confrontation. Some have even called me arrogant. It would seem that the stars (and their interpreters) have come eerily close to the mark.

But let's conduct an experiment. Allow me to post the attributes of another, non-Aries astrological sign so we can see what hits the target, and what hits the fan.

The ninth sign of the zodiac, Sagittarius, falls a full seven months after my birthday, and according to the same website, here's how Sagittarius would shake out for me:

I am represented by the archer, which is also a Centaur (half man, half beast). I am a wanderer in search of truth. I am a clear thinker, keenly interested in philosophy and religion. I devour information. I seek the meaning of life. I am a Big Picture person. I am optimistic, generous, just and noble. I become impatient and difficult when hemmed in. I'm outspoken. I'm a fast talker. I'm athletic and enjoy sports. I have a tendency to procrastinate. I'm a social creature. I am ruled by Jupiter, King of the Gods. My symbol is the arrow. My element is fire.

Again, I'm struck by how close (at least in my own mind) this particular archer came to the bullseye. I'm not athletic, but I'm a fun, social, outgoing guy in search of truth. I'm fascinated by religion. I can procrastinate. And I need plenty of breathing room. It's uncanny!

What's happening here is called the Forer Effect (also known as the Barnum Effect). Named for psychologist Bertram R. Forer, it refers to the tendency of people to rate this kind of information as highly accurate for them personally even though it could easily apply to a wide range of people.

In the 1940s, Forer gave a series of personality tests to his students, but he completely ignored their answers and simply passed out a canned evaluation (compiled from various horoscopes), with each student receiving the exact same description, which said the following:[110]

> **You have a need for other people to like and admire you, and yet you tend to be critical of yourself. While you have some personality weaknesses, you are generally able to compensate for them. You have considerable unused capacity that you have not turned to your advantage. Disciplined and self-controlled on the outside, you tend to be worrisome and insecure on the inside. At times you have serious doubts as to whether you have made the right decision or done the right thing. You prefer a certain amount of change and variety and become dissatisfied when hemmed in by restrictions and limitations. You also pride yourself as an independent thinker and do not accept others' statements without satisfactory proof. But you have found it unwise to be too frank in revealing yourself to others. At times you are extroverted, affable and sociable, while at other times you are introverted, wary and reserved. Some of your aspirations tend to be rather unrealistic. Security is one of your major goals in life.**

After distributing the evaluations to each student, Forer asked each of them to rate the evaluation on an accuracy scale from zero to five, with five being the most accurate. The class average was 4.26, meaning that students having different personalities each felt that this rubber-stamped profile was 84% accurate in describing themselves. The test has been repeated hundreds of times over the decades since, and the rating average continues to hover right around 4.26. The "facts" in

110 Forer, B.R. "The fallacy of personal validation: A classroom demonstration of gullibility". *Journal of Abnormal and Social Psychology.* American Psychological Association. Vol. 44 (1): pages 118–123. 1949. Web.

the personality evaluation are specific enough to appear tailored for the individual, but are actually generic and vague enough to apply to many. This is the Forer Effect at work, and it's easily exposed in my Aries/Sagittarius experiment above. A related phenomenon is "subjective validation," which happens as completely random and unrelated things are perceived to be connected when our own predispositions earnestly seek that connection. We actually lean forward into an expected result, and as such, horoscopes designed for the masses can seem hand-written specifically for us.[111]

A gentleman named David McCandless actually studied 22,168 horoscopes from the Yahoo.com astrology website, "Shine," and discovered that the key terms used for each horoscope were 90% identical to all of the others. On his website informationisbeautiful.net, McCandless actually used those common punch words to create a generic, meta prediction that would apply to pretty much everyone:[112]

> **"Ready? Sure? Whatever the situation or secret moment, enjoy everything a lot. Feel able to absolutely care. Expect nothing else. Keep making love. Family and friends matter. The world is life, fun and energy. Maybe hard. Or easy. Taking exactly enough is best. Help and talk to others. Change your mind and a better mood comes along..."**

Let's get back to the psychics who actually speak with paying customers about their destiny. Obviously, some patrons walk away from a session convinced that supernatural forces revealed or explained some very specific, often very personal and private information. Days later, they remain in awe of the psychic's abilities, obsessed with the nagging question, "How could they KNOW that?"

111 Marks, David F. *The Psychology of the Psychic*. 2 ed. Amherst, New York: Prometheus Books. 2000. Page 41. Web.
112 McCandless, David. "Horoscoped". *Information is Beautiful*. 19 January 2011. Web.

If you are that person, chances are that you've just been introduced to a tactic called "cold reading." There are whole books on the subject (I recommend Ian Rowland's, "The Full Facts Book of Cold Reading"), but the short explanation is this: Professional manipulators (sales-people, hypnotists, faith healers, con men, psychics, etc) play off of the gullibility of a willing subject, using word tricks, perception and conditioned response to imbue their revelations and predictions with more meaning than they actually have. They set the stage with the proper atmosphere and props. They demonstrate a warm, sympathetic demeanor. And they lead the unsuspecting mark exactly where he or she wishes to go.

Cold reading often involves several common elements.

1) **Fishing for the details**. The psychic says, "I'm sensing a name that starts with the letter M." At this point, as the subject, you begin flipping through a mental Rolodex. If your own name doesn't start with "M," you latch onto a sibling, grandparent, friend or other associate. The connection isn't made by the psychic, but by you. ("Yes! I have an uncle named Marty!") If no one with an "M" name comes to mind, the psychic simply deflects with something like, "Well, you've repressed a very important memory having to do with a person named 'M'." Or perhaps they were simply referring to your mother. See how that works?

2) **Keeping it vague**. The medium tosses out a series of generalities like, "You've been having doubts about a specific person lately. Is that right?" Now, the whole planet can be mined to fill in that gap. Perhaps you've had doubts about a life partner or friend, or perhaps you have doubts about the current president of Egypt. It doesn't matter. The psychic draws the box, and you fill it.

Another example might be the declaration that "An older man has been very influential to you." Eager to connect that dot, you mine the memory banks for a father, grandfather, uncle, older friend, neighbor, boss or associate, and you volunteer to the medium information that was never actually predicted. The psychic takes the ball you just handed him and runs with it.

3) **<u>Studying your appearance and gestures</u>**. You are a broadcast tower of "tells." Your language, posture, skin color, pupil dilation, breathing patterns, hand movements, expressions and quirks provide cues for the psychic to adjust, rephrase, elaborate, or course-correct. Your reaction to a claim feeds back to the medium like a sonar ping, allowing him to either capitalize on a "hit" or tap dance around a "miss."

Also, your personal appearance can provide plenty of clues to the observer. Are you athletic? Do you have a tan? What colors do you like to wear? Do you match or clash? Do you wear ornate, minimal or expensive jewelry? Is your hair meticulously coiffed, or mussed and matted? Do you have dirty fingernails? Your outer self can be a flashing billboard about your lifestyle, career, affluence and personality.

4) **"<u>Shotgunning.</u>"** The psychic unleashes a barrage of claims or questions in the hopes of hitting the target, and experienced, trained psychics can volley several hundred questions an hour. It's often overwhelming to the subject, who's trying to keep up, and in that context, only a few hits are necessary to foster the perception of accuracy. In fact, according to experts like Ian Rowland, James Randi, Derren Brown and others, an eager mark is likely to forget or ignore wrong guesses by a psychic (this is known as "selective thinking"), focusing almost completely on the correct guesses, filled with awe and wonder at his clairvoyant ability.

Speaking of Derren Brown, I encourage you to seek out his television special, "Trick of the Mind," which, at least at the time of this writing, is available on YouTube in the USA. In one segment, Brown uses cold reading techniques to (miraculously!) read the minds of college students, and his ability to manipulate the crowd is mesmerizing. One can easily see how a trained cold reader could win over the hearts, minds and wallets of an unsuspecting public.

5) **Condition your audience.** James Underdown at the Center for Inquiry did some research on John Edward, psychic star of the television show "Crossing Over with John Edward," and he discovered that Edward gave each of his audience members an eight-page advance letter encouraging them to mentally focus on significant dates, family members, even pets, with one section actually titled, "Recommended things to think about."[113]

And of course, television psychics also have their helpers in the editing room who are happy to ensure that any uncomfortable misses or failures never make it to broadcast.

There are "warm readings," where mediums actually have some vague information about their subjects in advance. There are "hot readings," where specific data is retrieved by informers and investigators, a process made even simpler through the use of online services which can scan everything from family data to medical histories to arrest reports. And there are many other weapons in the psychic arsenal.[114]

But could I ever fall prey to one of these operatives of the otherworld?

---

113 Underdown, Jim. "They See Dead People - Or Do They?: An Investigation of Television Mediums". *Skeptical Inquirer.* Vol 27.5. 2003. Web.

114 "Cold Reading", "Warm Reading" and "Hot Reading. *The Skeptic's Dictionary.* Edited by Carroll, Robert Todd. 12 September 2014. Web.

It was on my birthday in 2014 that I decided to dip my own toe into the waters of divination. I was spending the weekend in Ocean Beach, California, and for my birthday present, I asked Natalie to schedule a reading with a psychic in the area.

It didn't take long to find one. In California, they grow psychics on trees.

The establishment was in a business center (which should tell you something), complete with books, crystals, powders, potions, tarot cards, and even a black cat meandering around between the patrons. The place didn't feel mystical or magical, but more like a Saturday morning yard sale. People were quietly thumbing through the wares, most dressed for the beach, and there was a matter-of-factness about the establishment that stood in stark contrast to the dark, fabric-adorned rooms I'd seen in television and film. This wasn't a reverent theater for conducting spiritual energy. This was a pawn shop with talismans.

I had an entourage in tow - my then-fiancé (now wife) and some members of her family, and as I'm an atheist, I'm sure they were secretly nervous that I'd say or do something embarrassing. We approached the register, introduced ourselves and were directly whisked into a small room where the psychic, seated at the reading table, was finishing up a phone call.

She was a slight, dark-haired woman in her 50s (I'll call her Carol) dressed in a sleeveless sun dress that punctuated her tiny frame. She wrapped a lovely English accent around a rich alto voice, creating a feeling of happy displacement, like we'd been whisked from Ocean Beach to a suburb of Hogwarts.

Warm and pleasant, Carol smiled and invited us in. I took the point position at the table in the center of the room. Everyone else took chairs behind me. The round table supported an arsenal of psychic tools: cards, beads, stones, and the obligatory crystal ball. (The ball was unusual. I expected the standard clear glass, but this orb contained strange, flat patterns of distortion, and looking through it was like gazing through laser-etched quartz. Mesmerizing.)

The table also contained a tip jar.

Carol began by asking me questions, and she was in full shotgun mode. Where was I from? Why was I there? What did I hope to discover or accomplish? Honestly, I hadn't really considered any of this, as I was thinking she'd just look into my eyes (and the crystal ball) and leap into a rapid-fire demonstration of psychic reporting. I was being interviewed and observed, and of course, this is the calling card of cold reading.

Pressed, I admitted that I was a bit burned out on my 10-year day job. What might a cold reader construe from that admission? Well, there's dissatisfaction. Restlessness. Frustration. Boredom. A desire for change.

She asked what my profession was, and I said "video producer." Aha! I'm creative. Expressive. A storyteller. Someone who likes to paint outside the lines. A person frustrated by narrow boundaries and strict rules. Somewhat technical. Engaged in the world.

She asked what I did to relax. I like to write. Non-fiction. Articles. Blogs. Books. From this, she could latch onto the observational, contemplative communicator. She was painting my portrait, but I provided the outline and colors.

From that foundation, using a series of tarot cards bearing the likenesses of God, goddesses, wizards, druids, etc, she constructed an elaborate (and quite impressive) series of claims, and her "hits" were compelling. She spoke about a co-worker of mine with uncanny clarity, especially given the fact that the co-worker was my ex-wife ("There's a female you feel compelled to help in some way"). Carol then built on the author angle, declaring that I'd ultimately segue into more of a full-time writing role (Does this book fulfill her prophecy?). She expressed concern that I wasn't really happy, which at the time was probably apparent on my face, as I was burned out, tired and struggling with a health issue.

In many ways, she seemed to know me. It's easy to see how someone might be easily swept into this feeling of connection and empathy. Her predictions and claims "hit" so often.

But unlike many, I was also well aware of the misses.

Carol spoke of a future partnership with a woman that would propel me to career success. This, of course, placed no burden of accuracy upon the psychic, as my ass would be 1,500 miles away if the prediction never came true. She also referred to a future love interest, which was awkward, seeing as how my fiancé was sitting directly behind me. And her references to God (a nebulous being she spoke about only in generalities) fell flat, especially when I informed her that I do not believe in a Higher Power. In fact, at that revelation, she tossed the God tarot card completely out of the stack and continued my reading without it.

Do I think Carol is a charlatan and a con artist? Who knows? Certainly, the best snake oil salesmen appear sincere and genuine, but it's highly possible that this woman simply drank deep from this world's vast wellspring of woo.

Ultimately, I remain the skeptic. I doubt that those in rags can point others to riches, nor do I think that the psychic 1% are genuinely interested in helping people by fleecing them for $400 an hour. I think crystals are for decoration and cards are for poker. I want published biographies and credentials for every person who writes a horoscope. I'd like for CNN to post a weekly highlight reel for every major failed psychic prediction. I'd like a disclaimer on the door of every palm reader, card reader, medium and mentalist which reads, "For Entertainment Purposes Only." And I'm convinced that the true crystal ball on the psychic's table is the tip jar filled with dollar bills, exchanging funds for fortune-teller fiction, even as the raindrops leak through the chipped shingles above her head.

CHAPTER 9
The Penis Parade

I have a confession. The word "penis" makes me uncomfortable.

You must understand that I was raised in a hugely conservative home. We didn't speak of sex, and by default, we didn't speak about body parts that might one day find themselves engaged in sex. Like sleeping giants, they were not to be called by name, lest they awaken and run amok.

Ever see the M. Night Shyamalan film, "The Village," where the residents of a puritan town refer to the forest monsters as "Those We Don't Speak Of?" That's exactly how religious parents approach conversations about the penis and vagina. Even when they talk about it… they don't talk about it.

My parents were experts at referring to genitalia with every word EXCEPT the clinical definition. Those uncomfortable conversations either revolved around "It" or "That," or they would end with mom or dad awkwardly pointing below the belt and saying, "You know… down *there!*"

I've heard similar stories from many of my peers who remember parental references to things like "girl bits" and "boy parts." One mother attempted to educate a daughter about her "plum." Some pre-adolescent boys adopted the classic nicknames, "Wee Wee," "Pee Pee," "Weiner," "Weenie," and in a few unfortunate cases, "Penie."

In many houses, the word "dick" caused discomfort, even when accurately used to address someone by their actual name. ("Your name's Dick? Mind if I call you Richard?") And of course, no self-respecting parent would use such a crude term when talking to little Timmy about why he shouldn't draw eyeballs on the tip of his penie.

When you stop to think about it, the word "penis" solves a lot of problems. Merriam-Webster's own definition says this:

pe·nis

noun \ˈpē-nəs\
: the part of the body of men and male animals that is
used for sex and through which urine leaves the body

Yes! That's exactly what it is, and that's exactly what it does. But for some reason, I've grown up in a culture which rejects this word in favor of monikers like Man Candle, Baby Maker, Excalibur, Junk, Boomstick, Tallywhacker, Schlong, Schnitzel, Pecker, Private Eye, Willy, Longfellow, Dragon and (a personal favorite) Krull the Warrior King.

The whole damn country has a problem with a legitimate term describing an organic part of a naturally healthy body. We've got to get over our Problem with the Penis!

Perhaps the USA could take a cue from Kawasaki, Japan, which not only embraces the penis (providing dozens of opportunities for double entendres), but parades it *literally* down the street!

Every year during the first week of April, Kawasaki is the scene of an ancient Shinto festival called, "Kanamara Matsuri," which translates (and I'm not kidding), "Festival of the Steel Penis." A tradition since the 1600s, this week-long party was apparently borne of a legend about a virgin girl and a dirty demon with an appetite for destruction. Here's the story:

An innkeeper's daughter was about to get married. However, an evil demon heard about the nuptials and, because the woman had previously refused the demon's advances and instead married a human male, he decided to ruin the party by finding the bride-to-be and crawling into her vagina. (Stay with me. It gets even more bizarre.) Afraid to tell anyone about the gargoyle in her girly-bits, she proceeded with the marriage ceremony and retreated with her new husband to consummate the marriage.

Unfortunately for the man, the demon lurking inside his wife had worked up quite the appetite, resulting in one of the most horrifying accounts of castration imaginable. And he wasn't the only victim, as a later suitor also found himself in the honeymoon suite being violently parted from his pork.

Enter a new character in this story: the blacksmith. A clever man who had heard about this demon under the dress, he devised an ingenious solution. He cast a penis made of iron and tricked the demon, who bit down sharply upon cold metal and fled the town humiliated.

The woman and the blacksmith married, and the enormous iron shrine at the Kanamara Matsuri is said to mark the day that evil was vanquished by true love, quick thinking and an unbreakable boner.

Today, this festival is hugely popular with both residents and tourists. Lighthearted and rich with good humor, the event begins with the lighting of the secret flame. After this ceremony, a huge pink phallus is carried around the city by a group of transvestites. Small souvenir penises are available for sale, and visitors are encouraged to rub them against the nearby vagina sculpture to bring about good luck.

Good luck is much of what Kanamara Matsuri is about, as the region once hosted travelers and traders in "tea houses" (which often entertained guests with much more than tea), and the Shinto prostitutes used the penis shrine to ask for protection from sexually-transmitted diseases. When the shrine became portable, the festival was born.[115]

You might find it odd that the parade and festivities aren't just enjoyed by adults. Children's faces can be seen throughout the crowds. Yes, there are symbols of sexuality everywhere, but the occasion isn't about sex acts, and the statues simply reflect a frank and unashamed attitude toward the body parts they represent. The atmosphere is light, fun and festive. Gift shops sell things like penis-shaped lollipops and fake noses. And in the modern day, Kanamara Matsuri has evolved to not

---

115 "Kanamara Matsuri 2014: What You Should Know About Japan's Penis Festival". *The Huffington Post, Canada*. 7 April 2014. Web.

only honor fertility, but to also raise awareness about STDs and raise money for HIV research.[116]

Go figure. A city in Japan has conquered the shame of the schlong. And while it has perhaps the creepiest backstory in history, the tradition of Kanamara Matsuri does provide a terrific example of how to undo a taboo. While our parents and grandparents clumsily dodge the dreaded "P" word, a city in Japan prepares to boldly lift a giant, pink penis to the sky.

It's an erection that must be seen to be believed.

---

116 "Dammit, we missed The Festival of the Steel Phallus in Japan this weekend". *Cosmopolitan Magazine*. 7 April 2014. Web.

CHAPTER 10
Santa's Little Helper

Is there a fluffier, more benign, less threatening and generally happier holiday icon than Santa Claus? He's rounder and jollier than the Easter Bunny. His sleigh flies higher and faster than any 4th of July mortar, its shimmering glow provided by a 1,000-watt reindeer nose. Where Halloween brings the crimson red of vampire blood and the arterial spray of countless slasher flicks, the eve of December 24th brings the bright, cherry red of Santa's coat and trousers.

Santa Claus makes people happy.

He certainly makes department stores happy. In fact, our collective mental image of Saint Nicholas is largely the product of retail advertising.

Saint Nick is based on an actual Saint (Nicholas of Myra), a 4th century Christian bishop who was famous for giving gifts to poor people. In death, he became the patron saint of numerous groups (including children), and his growing legend (possibly colored by pagan influences, specifically the Norse god, Odin) ultimately came to incorporate a long, white beard and flying horses, the stallions later exchanged for reindeer in North America.[117]

---

117 Handwerk, Brian. "St. Nicholas to Santa: The Surprising Origins of Mr. Claus". *National Geographic*. 20 December 2013. Web.

The name, back story and details varied from culture to culture over the centuries, but "Santa Claus" was ultimately Americanized from the Dutch "Sinterklaas," and Clement Moore's famous 1823 poem (now known as "'Twas The Night Before Christmas") branded the image of a chimney-crawling, rosy-cheeked, white-bearded, pipe-smoking fat guy into the collective brains of a generation.

Cartoonist Thomas Nast cemented Santa in ink with his now-famous 1860s illustrations published in Harper's Weekly, and early 20th century retailers like Coca-Cola plastered Nast's version of Jolly Ol' Saint Nick on their products, forever marrying Christmas with commerce and guaranteeing that Wal-Mart, Target and Macy's would be eagerly stocking shelves with Santa-themed merchandise as early as September.[118]

I'll admit that the billion-dollar Christmas industry has jaded the once sentimental kid inside me. One of my earliest jobs was in retail, and every November/December would bring a frothing mob of credit-card-wielding zombies who crowded, rushed, pushed, fought, cried, shouted and generally embarrassed themselves over some trinket that would ultimately die a slow, dark, lonely death in somebody's trash can.

---

118 Forbes, Bruce D. *Christmas: A Candid History*. University of California Press. 2008. p. 89. Print.

Right now, you're nodding your head, because you can immediately compile a mental list of once-hot Christmas gifts that transformed otherwise rational people into hair-pulling thugs: Cabbage Patch Kids, Nintendo, Furby, GoBots, Teddy Ruxpin, Pokemon, My Little Ponies, Pogs, Bratz, Barney, Razor Scooters, Beanie Babies, Tamagochi, Tickle Me Elmo, etc. Year after year, the sheeple would catch a whiff of whatever craze was blowing in the wind, and they'd cast off their own families on Thanksgiving so they could sleep at the entrance of the nearest retail crap-trap until some red-vested minion showed up to unlock the door.

These days, the stores don't even bother to close, so the purchasing public can debase itself even sooner. And the ringmaster for this circus is Santa Claus. He's everywhere. Santa figurines. Santa wrapping paper. Santa gift cards. Santa picture frames. Santa cupcakes. Santa sweaters. Santa popcorn tins. Santa jewelry. Santa candles. Santa ornaments. Santa inflatables. Even the Salvation Army bell ringer is dressed up as Santa.

Yet somehow, despite the fact that he's constantly paraded before us in this fashion, the character of Santa Claus has managed to escape the ire of most holiday cynics, and he remains absolutely adored by children. Each December, Santa brings only smiles, only goodness, only a Ho-Ho-Ho and a holly-jolly Christmas. He is the kindest, gentlest, most benign old gentleman in the world, and even the naughtiest of children would never have to fear him, right?

Wrong. Allow me to introduce you to Santa's little helper…from Hell.

Christmas tradition in Austria, Northern Italy and other parts of Europe has Saint Nicholas visiting eager children with a dark companion in tow: a horned, cloven-hoofed demon called the Krampus.[119] Forget threatening naughty kids with lumps of coal in their stockings.

119 Crimmins, Peter. "Horror For The Holidays: Meet The Anti-Santa". *National Public Radio.* 10 December 2011, 2:34am ET. Web.

The Krampus will make them sorry they were ever born.

The legend of the Krampus spans thousands of years and, like Santa, also has roots in ancient pagan symbolism and Germanic folklore. [120] He's a nasty creature, tall and imposing, often covered in dark hair and flicking the air with a large, pointed tongue. He carries rusty chains[121] and slings a large sack[122] across his back (and I'll get back to those).

If you're a fan of J.R.R. Tolkien, imagine the Krampus as a Christmas Balrog, and if he ever pops down your chimney, you're guaranteed to have at least one less child to shop for next year.

---

120 Strasbaugh, Jessie. "German holiday traditions: the Krampus". *Oxford Dictionaries*. 4 December 2012. Web.

121 Basu, Tanya. "Who Is Krampus? Explaining the Horrific Christmas Devil". *National Geographic*. 19 December 2013. Web.

122 See Footnote 120.

Let's explore a scenario where a family's youngest son (let's call him Timmy) marks an entire year with spoiled, disobedient and rebellious behavior. While his older siblings toe the line and earn their Christmas visit from Saint Nick, Timmy does not.

Well, apparently, Santa thinks that kids like Timmy need to be taught a lesson, but he doesn't like to do his own dirty work, so on December 5th (the eve of Saint Nicholas' Day), Santa rushes off for an evening of gifts, merriment, milk and cookies with the good children, tasking his pet demon to serve up a "naughty list" recipe of pain and death for everyone who fell short of the mark.[123] Little Timmy is in for a long night.

According to legend, the Krampus will drop by Timmy's house with rusty chain in hand and flog the child mercilessly. Once the boy has been soundly beaten, the demon will cram his still-living body into the sack and, depending on region and tradition, do one of the following:

1.) Feast upon his flesh.

2.) Toss him in the river to drown.

3.) Drag him down into the fiery pit of Hell.

It's pretty obvious why an American public weaned on "A Charlie Brown Christmas" isn't spinning this gruesome yarn around the hearth. (*"Santa Claus is comin' to town, kids. And his demon will fuck you up."*) But in places like Austria, Romania, Bavaria, Hungary, Croatia and the Czech Republic, the Krampus is so adored that Krampustag ("Krampus Day") is celebrated with huge and elaborate parades. Hundreds of spectators wait in the streets for the ominous sound

---

123 See Footnote 120.

of rattling chains and rusty cowbells announcing the arrival of the Krampusse, packs of costumed men adorned in animal fur, wooden masks, tall horns and glowing red eyes. As the crowd shouts in terror and delight, it is taunted and teased by Hell's minions. Females join in the taunting disguised as Frau Bercht, fire-breathing black angels, and there are even mini-demons played by children.[124]

It's a wild, happy, scary, surreal affair, perfect for those who wish that Halloween had an encore. And for the sensitive and squeamish, softer versions of the Krampus figure can be found (picture the offspring of a Valentine's cupid and Hellboy).

Of course, the Krampus isn't the only Christmas icon with pagan roots. Christmas trees hearken back to the ancient Winter Solstice traditions of using evergreen boughs to honor the gods of the sun and agriculture, and offerings were made to deities like Baldur and Ra for a bountiful spring harvest. The Winter Solstice also helps to explain December 25th as the selected date for Christmas, as eager celebrants yearned for the return of the sun[125] (not the Son, incidentally). Gift exchange stems back to the Festival of Saturnalia, honoring Saturn, the Roman god of agriculture. The practice of burning Yule logs is said to have pagan origins, referring to a Nordic winter festival with celebrants drinking around a large fire. Yes, as millions of Christians welcome traditions like these into their homes and hearts, they're largely unaware that, even if they're skipping the whole Krampus thing, they are still practicing traditions rooted in paganism.

Interestingly, there are tiny blips of Krampus celebrations in the United States, but for now, it seems that Santa's happy, harmless reputation

124 Crosby, Alexandra. "Devils and maidens: Austria's Krampus parades". *NineMSN Travel.* Undated. Web.
125 Van Luling, Todd. "Everything You Know About Christmas Is Wrong". *The World Post, via The Huffington Post.* 9 December 2013. Web.
    a.   "Winter Solstice". *BBC.* 7 April 2006. Web.

is largely safe in this part of the world. He still knows if you've been bad or good (so be good for goodness' sake!), but the only real consequence will be fewer boxes under the tree. No demon. No chains. No whips. No drowning sacks. No rendezvous with Satan in Hades. The only red you'll see will be the bright, brilliant, ruby glow of flashing Christmas lights.

However, if you've got a troublesome youngster in the house and you'd like to take a "scared straight" approach to behavior modification, perhaps this variation on Clement Moore will straighten the spine of your insolent sprout and make the choice between "naughty" and "nice" a bit clearer:

'Twas the night before Christmas, and all through the house
Ran a sniveling, back-talking, spoiled little louse.
His parents were thwarted at every attempt
And threw up their hands at his sneering contempt.

But now he prepared for the gifts he would savor
Despite a full year of substandard behavior.
He watched near the hearth for the dangling of boots
And Santa's big bag with a shit-ton of loot.

But much to his horror, he didn't see feet
The fireplace ignited with billows of heat.
The room turned to crimson, the air turned to steam
And a demon emerged with a deafening scream.

It grappled and dangled and rattled its chain
The scourge of Saint Nick, an announcement of pain.
Along with the stomping of hooves on the floor
And glowing red eyes that were vile to the core.

The Krampus had come with a present indeed
But one borne of avarice, defiance and greed.
It bellowed with laughter, it teased and it taunted
And as the boy begged, it continued undaunted.

The striking, the whipping, the snap of the chain
Until just a shell of the boy would remain.
Then promptly, it brandished a bag from its back
And stuffed the child into the large empty sack.

To drag it and carry it into a well
That emptied way down in the chasm of Hell.

With devils and demons and writhing and fire
And Satan's throne perched high atop the red mire.

Oh, how this young boy wished he'd lived his life better
And followed instructions right down to the letter.
If he could go back, he would fix his mistakes
And undo his crimes with whatever it takes.

He'd listen and speak with respect and concern
He'd say "please" and "thank you" at every turn.
He'd cook and he'd clean and he'd make up his bed
Deferring and nodding and bowing his head.

Alas, all his chances to change and revoke
Have gone in a plume of red ash, fire and smoke.
The Krampus came calling to do Santa's bidding
He'd told kids "Be good," and he sure wasn't kidding.

So listen, dear children, and don't you forget
That which you've given, you surely will get.
Will you get the carrot, will you get the stick
Will you meet the Krampus, will you meet Saint Nick?

Ol' Santa is watching and you're on the clock
And youngsters across this great planet, take stock.
December will come and your measure be taken
So act like a saint or your ass will be bacon.

Merry Christmas.

CHAPTER 11
Rise Up and Walk!

scha·den·freu·de[126]

noun, *often capitalized* \ˈshä-dᵊn-ˌfroi-də\
: a feeling of enjoyment that comes from seeing or
hearing about the troubles of other people

I've experienced Schadenfreude. The year was 1986, televangelism was huge, and a fast-talking faith healer named Peter Popoff was cruising the country, promising miracles and passing the plate to the tune of a $4 million annual salary.[127] His healing services saw packed houses of hope-starved (and often gravely ill) followers desperate to be whole again. Popoff not only claimed to have God's ear, but also the divine power to destroy cancer, restore useless limbs and set the physically and spiritually captive free.

In my opinion, you could construct an effigy of Peter Popoff made of Crisco, banana peels and jojoba oil, and it would still be less slick than the original.

His services were pure theater. Big music. Big gestures. Big promises.

---

126 "Schadenfreude, n." *Merriam Webster Dictionary Online*. Encyclopedia Britannica, 2015. Web.
127 "Secrets of the Psychics". *NOVA*. October 19, 1993

Big hair. From the stage, Popoff miraculously rattled off the names of random audience members, their home addresses, their ailments, the specific details of their lives, obviously channeling the omniscient eye of the Almighty.

Thousands watched in amazement as he called individuals out to infuse them with the Holy Spirit. Popoff touched, grabbed, pushed, pulled, slapped, smacked and otherwise put the spank on Satan, the eager throng celebrating this incredible move of God. Attendees tossed their wheelchairs, crutches and walkers, striding the stage to thunderous applause. They threw their medications away and received the restoration of their physical temples. It was a purification, a manifestation, a revelation, a miracle.

Of course...Popoff was so full of shit, a single laxative would have caused him to disappear.

The famous illusionist and skeptic James Randi had been following Peter Popoff's crusade tour from city to city, working with electronics experts embedded in the audience to search for any sign of mischief. Using a scanner during a Popoff service in San Francisco, Randi and his assistant Alexander Jason discovered the voice of God...which sounded suspiciously like Pete's wife reading prayer cards into a microphone. It seems that Popoff was receiving cues from his bride via a tiny earpiece receiver he'd passed off as a "hearing aid" (why the hell would a faith healer need a hearing aid?), and when Randi went public with the information, Peter Popoff spiraled from protest to admission to humiliation to bankruptcy within the course of a year.[128]

It was beautiful.

---

128 See Footnote 127
    a.   Randi, James. *The Faith Healers*. Prometheus Books. 1989. Pages 2, 147. Print.

A glow of satisfaction surrounded me. A warm, gooey sense of justice welled within me. Schadenfreude enveloped me. A charlatan had been put down, and this slimy con could no longer build a life of luxury and celebrity upon the gullible masses...right?

Put this book down for a moment and do a Google search for "Peter Popoff." At the top of the list, you'll find a still-thriving "ministry," promises of still-unproven miracles and, of course, requests for donations. His current net worth is unclear, as he switched his organization from "for profit" to "religious" in 2005,[129] but one look at his $4.5 million mansion in Bradbury, California, his Porsche, his Mercedes-Benz, and the 7-figure salary in place before he decided to play the church card on tax day, and it's pretty clear he's been riding the offering plate down Easy Street. Somehow, Peter Popoff remains a television celebrity and a sought-after agent of healing power. In fact, Business Insider did a 2011 article on Popoff titled, "Scam Everlasting."

In 2007, out of sheer morbid curiosity, a co-worker of mine named Morgan (who's actually a devout Christian and despises Popoff) sent in a request for prayer to his current ministry, "People United for Christ." Within days, she received a long, pre-printed letter covered in blue-inked "notes" deceptively formatted to appear handwritten by Peter Popoff himself. The letter promised financial "blessings" if she would place a penny under a glass of water by her bedside. How this unleashes the financial windfall is still unclear, and it's far from the most bizarre of instructions given out by the Popoff camp. Other recipients have posted online screenshots of PUFC letters declaring that a "bracelet of blessing" would cause divine bank transfers to miraculously appear in their checking accounts (no idea how that would look on a monthly statement). Others have received small packets of "miracle spring water" which

---

129 Maag, Christopher. "Scam Everlasting: After 25 Years, Debunked Faith Healer Still Preaching Debt Relief Scam". *Business Insider.* 22 September 2011. Web.

allegedly possess the power to wash away debt.

Morgan never did try the penny-by-the-bedside stunt, and subsequent letters from Popoff's organization (all pleading for money) became so frequent that she had to write "return to sender / occupant no longer lives here" on the envelope before the barrage finally ended.

I personally attempted the penny-under-a-glass method, yet to date, I am not wealthy. Popoff, however, probably stuffs his mattress with social security checks sent in by the gullible masses who haven't stopped to wonder why a prosperity prophet is having to shake other people down for cash.

And Peter Popoff is a drop in the bucket. Those of us raised in or around Christian evangelists are familiar with the silk-suited, jewel-adorned rock stars of Gawd's POW-ah: Benny Hinn. T.L. Osborne. Kathryn Kuhlman. Robert Tilton. Kenneth Copeland. W. V. Grant. Paul and Jan Crouch. In my own backyard, evangelist Oral Roberts rose from revival tent preacher to the president of his own, faith-based university. He also founded the City of Faith hospital, which seems an odd project for someone claiming the ability to heal the sick on a wing and a prayer.

To the eager and uninitiated, the tricks of the faith healer can seem quite impressive, yet they've been exposed by a host of debunkers and even former evangelists. There's the "lengthening the leg" miracle, which has the healer subtly sliding the heel of one's shoe to emulate a growing limb. There's the selection of someone in the audience who's sitting next to a pair of crutches, the "rise and walk" command astounding those who didn't realize that the crutches actually belonged to the poor guy sitting in the next chair. Healers often place fully-ambulatory patrons in wheelchairs long before the show. Evangelists magnify minor maladies into major ones so the healing effect is compounded ("Only moments ago, this woman could barely walk!"). Some use crib sheets, hand signals, code words or, like Popoff, prayer cards and electronic transmitters to "know" the specifics of a person's circumstance or condition. Many do "cold reading," the bread and butter for psychics (covered in another chapter in this book). There's the shotgun approach, where the healer announces that many unnamed people in the audience are simultaneously being cured of a specific disease. "Blind" people given sight are often not completely blind and actually possess limited vision, so their post-miracle navigation of stages and stairs is easily explainable. And healers sometimes imbue the ailing with a whiz-bang dose of divine power using hypnosis cues or (in what's known as the "low tackle" approach) even physically pushing them to the floor. This is often called being "slain in the spirit," and as the body faints from this injection of the Holy Ghost, ushers or assistants stand ready to catch the falling faithful and lay them softly onto the ground.

"Softly onto the ground." Remember that phrase as I recount the case of Matthew Lincoln, who attended a healing service at Lakewind Church in Knox County, Tennessee in hopes of finding relief from a spinal condition. When minister Robert Lavala touched Lincoln's forehead and called down divine power, the afflicted man *received the spirit* and fell backwards. Unfortunately, somebody forgot to put the ushers in the catcher position, and this freshly-slain believer did not fall "softly onto the ground." In fact, Matthew (and his already-torqued spine) crashed against the thinly-carpeted concrete floor like a doomed skydiver. Cue the attorneys and a $2.5 million lawsuit against the church.[130] God, to date, hasn't shown up in court as a witness.

And while we're on the subject of Christian healers, believe it or not, there's a guy named Tyler Johnson who founded a group called "The Dead Raising Team (DRT)." He claims to pray for the dead and

---

130 "Man Falls After Receiving Spirit, Sues". *The Smoking Gun*. 5 June 2008. Web.

bring about the resurrection of lifeless bodies. A graduate of Bethel's School of Supernatural Ministry[131] (which is, surprise, a church!), Johnson has yet to provide hard evidence that he possesses the power to reanimate corpses, which is unfortunate, as that kind of thing would be of great interest to all grieving funeral-goers and the Nobel Prize committee.

For those outside the narrow walls of the Christian church, there are plenty of other options for diagnosis and healing. Allow me to introduce you to Hogen Fukenaga, the charismatic founder of Japan's Ho No Hana Sanpogyo cult[132] which gained popularity in the 1980s. Fukenaga claims he is the reincarnation of Jesus Christ and Buddha, and he tells his followers (estimated at over 30,000 members during the cult's heyday)[133] that he can diagnose sickness by examining their feet. The price tag? $900 per reading. Some individuals have paid over $900,000 to ensure their continued good health. (Accused of swindling a host of housewives in the '90s, Fukenaga was forced to pay over $2 million in damages, yet his "ministry" continues.)

At Santuario de Chimayo, just north of Sante Fe, New Mexico, it's believed that the dirt has healing powers. The sick and afflicted from around the world have been known to take pilgrimages to this sacred spot, but if you can't make the trek, do not despair. Holy dirt can be shipped to you for free (although donations are welcome, of course), and you're instructed to simply pray and "rub the Holy Dirt over the part of your body in need of healing." The El Santuario de Chimayo website is clear in its warning that YOU ARE NOT TO EAT THE DIRT.[134] Wait. This is a problem?

---

131 "The Dead Raising Team Founder". *The Dead Raising Team.* 2015. Web.
      a.   "Bethel School of Supernatural Ministry". http://bssm.net. 2015. Web.
132 Getzlaff, J.A. "Japanese court throws book at foot cult". *Salon.* 9 May 2000. Web.
133 "Leaders of foot cult arrested". *BBC News.* 9 May 2000. Web.
134 "Holy Dirt Request". *El Santuario de Chimayo.* 2013. Web.

And dirt certainly isn't the only element infused with healing energy. One needs only to glance at New Age healing practices to see that the instruments for wholeness surround us. A few examples of these "alternative" roads to good health:

- **HEALING WITH SOUND.**[135] Yes, each organ in the body is believed to have a corresponding vibration attached to it. You must recite the sacred words, chants or mantras to penetrate the psyche and align imbalanced energies which were created by the unnatural and unpleasant rumblings of the everyday world. Traffic noise, cell phone ring tones, television sets, barking dogs, slamming doors, power tools, car alarms, Justin Bieber...these hugely irritating sounds disrupt the harmonious rhythms of the inner you, and it's important to vibrate positively.

---

135 "Sound Healing Offerings". *Globe Institute Sound and Consciousness*. 2015. Web.

- **CHROMATHERAPY: HEALING WITH COLOR.**[136] Colors can correspond to different areas of the body. According to spiritualist and color guru, Charles W. Leadbeater, and his book, "Inner Life," the energy center at the base of your spine is orange, your solar plexus aura is green, the heart color is gold, the throat radiates a silvery blue, and the head is a palette of rose, yellow, blue, purple, gold and white. Surrounding yourself with colorful objects and imagining colors in your mind can unleash the rainbow for mental, physical and spiritual wellness.

- **HEALING CRYSTALS.** In Hinduism and other belief systems, "chakras" are energy points in the body that connect to the physical body. According to the website ChakraEnergy. com, there are no less than seven main chakra centers aligned along your spinal column. Placing certain crystals and/or stones over the correct chakra points (and other points of imbalance or spiritual blockage) can help to realign the body's energies.

- **EAV.**[137] EAV devices allegedly measure flow disruptions of your "electromagnetic energy" along "acupuncture meridians."[138] Again, it seems that you have some serious imbalances, and the EAV is supposed to measure the stresses, resonance and vibrations of your body's tissues and organs. (As most EAV devices, like the Scientology E-meters, are actually little more than meters for the electrical current that the body naturally generates, you're pretty much guaranteed to see some action on the dial.)

---

136 C. W. Leadbeater "Inner Life," Vol. 1, page 447-460, as cited by *Path of Light.Com.* 2015. Web.
137 Barrett, Stephen M.D. "Quack "Electrodiagnostic" Devices". *Quackwatch.* 7 July 2012. Web.
138 See Footnote 137.

- **REFLEXOLOGY.**[139] Also known as Zone Therapy, reflexology involves the act of applying pressure to parts of the feet and hands which correspond to your internal organs, glands and other parts of the body. With regard to the lower extremities, practitioners say that the toes are connected to the head, the ball of the foot relates to the heart and chest, the foot arch is tied to the liver, pancreas and kidney, and the heel links to the intestines and lower back. Treating maladies in those zones is apparently as simple as the proper application of pressure to the right portion of the foot. By this logic, one could potentially treat Alzheimer's by having a New Age guru poke them on the pinky toe.

- **POLARITY THERAPY.**[140] We're back to the electrical energy of the body. It seems you have both "plus" and "minus" energy, positive and negative energy, and when those forces are out of whack, you are imbalanced and require an alignment of polarity. The process involves physical touch, with the practitioner's hands placed on opposite sides of your body as he realigns the energies. When the process is finished, the therapist shakes his hands vigorously in the air to release any icky, negative energy he might have picked up from you. After all, he doesn't want to take any "neg vibes" home to the family.

- **AROMATHERAPY.**[141] Healing is made possible by breathing in the essential oil fragrances of flowers, herbs and aromatic woods, re-balancing the body, mind and spirit. Inhale. Exhale. Inhale. Exhale.

139 Bauer, Brent A., M.D. "What is reflexology? Can it relieve stress?". *Mayo Clinic*. 15 December 2012. Web.

140 Wilson ,Will. "Polarity Therapy: An Introduction". *American Polarity Therapy Association*. 2010. Web.

141 Aromatherapy.com - The Balance & Harmony of Body & Mind

- **READING YOUR AURA.**[142] Around each and every human body, there's an energy field that emits colors. This association is a bit different from Chromatherapy, as it speaks to single colors projected from the whole person. Grey is associated with negativity, fear and depression. Orange represents pride, boldness and ambition. Deep red is anger. Of course, in order to be able to observe the aura, you must be able to see into the spirit realm, which requires the awakening of your Sixth Sense, your Third Eye, the All-Seeing Eye. (Of course, when I think of the All-Seeing Eye, I think of Google.)

- **ASTRAL TRAVEL.**[143] Also known as astral projection, this out-of-body experience allows you to leave your physical form and travel into higher realms. Essentially, the soul goes on walkabout, and your altered state of consciousness galvanizes your true, spiritual self while moving you ever closer to the wholeness and purity of God. These journeys through space and time are occasionally initiated through the use of hallucinogenics, so you'll want to keep the peyote and mushrooms handy.

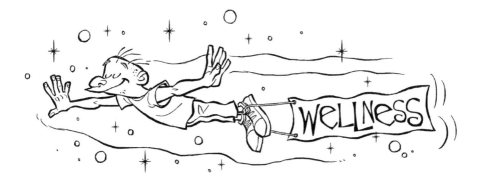

142 Oslie, Pam. "Quiz: What's Your Aura Color?". *The Dr. Oz Show.* 15 July 2014. Web.
143 Radford, Benjamin. "Astral Projection: Just a Mind Trip". *LiveScience.* 18 March 2013. Web.

It must be said that there are countless variations on these beliefs and practices, and each spiritual chef adds his/her own ingredients to the wellness recipe. But how solid is the science behind these uncommon cures? The Journal of the American Medical Association has studied the effectiveness of alternative medicine and found that a few remedies appear to provide positive health benefits. Yoga can apparently help with carpal tunnel syndrome. Spinal manipulation (chiropractic) may help with lower back pain. Tai Chi might help with fibromyalgia pain. Etc. But on the whole, the data on everything from acupuncture to homeopathy to energy alignment isn't flattering, and it's highly unlikely the AMA will ever encourage cancer patients to forego chemotherapy in favor of tuning forks, incense sticks and blue wallpaper.[144]

Besides, if alternative medicine was ever to be proven through peer-review, clinical trials and demonstrable results, it wouldn't be "alternative." It would be, simply, medicine. And are we genuinely prepared to discount the expertise of licensed, science-based physicians in favor of an unschooled homeopath whose main qualification is that he tattooed a third eye around his left nipple?

I suppose some of this stuff is better than the wares pitched by our ancestors. In ancient Mesopotamia, dentistry apparently involved the cosmological incantation of the "tooth worm."[145] Ancient Egyptians' remedy for tooth pain had them placing a dead rodent in your mouth. This bizarre practice was also supposed to treat measles, smallpox and whooping cough[146] (but not, apparently, funky breath). Less than 100 years ago, radium cures were prescribed for those seeking youthful vigor and potency in the bedroom, many packages of radioactive wa-

---

144 Briggs, Josephine P. MD; Jack Killen, MD. "Perspectives on Complementary and Alternative Medicine Research" *The Journal of the American Medical Association*. 21 August 2013. Web.

145 Belofsky, Nathan. *Strange Medicine: A Shocking History of Real Medical Practices Through the Ages*. New York: Perigee Books. 2013. Print.

146 Haviland, David. "15 Most Bizarre Medical Treatments Ever". *CBS News*. 2015. Web.

ter sold with an accompanying Geiger counter.[147] Asthma was once treated with powdered toads.[148] Acu-dots were magnetic Band Aids said to attract the iron in your blood, which allegedly increased circulation and helped with muscle and joint pain.[149] Versions and variations of these continue to be sold today. Alternative medicine does love its magnets.

Sure, we've advanced beyond bloodletting, heroin cough syrup and rubbing open wounds with mercury. Yet today, our Age of Enlightenment continues to see more than its fair share of weird and wild healing practices. The Terrapin turtle of Cambodia is said to cure rheumatism and other ailments with a single touch [150] (yes, if you consult a Cambodian healer, he just might rub a turtle on you). Psychic surgeons in the Philippines (for a fee) seem to miraculously thrust their bare hands into the bodies of patients, removing toxic "tissue" that looks exactly like fake blood, chicken guts and even bacon.[151] (Apparently, the people of the Philippines haven't yet discovered the cure for bullshit.) There's Urotherapy, which has patients self-treating for everything from acne to Psoriasis by drinking their own pee.[152] The famous Bathini Goud brothers of India treat thousands of patients for breathing problems by having them swallow a live murrel fish.[153] In Thailand, it's believed by many that you can cure any illness by drinking the blood of a snake.

The list goes on and on. As a supposedly enlightened and evolved

147 "Radium Cures". *Museum of Quackery.Com*. Undated. Web.
148 Wesley, John. "Primitive Physick, or An Easy and Natural Method of Curing Most Diseases". Republished by: *Golbal Ministries of the United Methodist Church*. Original Publication: 11 June 1747. Web.
149 "ACU-DOT magnetic analgesic patches". *Science Buzz, Science Museum of Minnesota*. 2015. Web.
150 "Weird Cures from Around the World". *Healthy Times Blog*. 21 December 2010. Web.
151 "Psychic 'Surgery'". *The Skeptic's Dictionary*. Edited by Carroll, Robert Todd. 12 September 2014. Web.
152 "Urotherapy – Exploration into Urine Therapy". *Urine Therapy*. 12 February 2015. Web.
153 "Bathini: Harbal (SIC) food supplement for Asthama (SIC) Patients". *Bathini Mrugasira Trust*. 2015. Web.

species, we continue to pin our hopes for good health on the faith healer, the shaman, pyramid power, sacred geometry, crystals, light, color, tunes, tones, potions, powders, smoke, mists, auras, oracles and magic wands. There's some research on the placebo effects and subsequent biochemical boosts that non-medicine "medicine" might provide, and I certainly wouldn't begrudge someone the right to think out of the box (as long as they don't climb to the top and leap to their doom). But I can only imagine how unbelievably frustrated doctors, nurses, pharmacists and scientists must become as they continually see distracted and desperate patients foregoing proven treatments to pin their hopes on unlicensed "healers" who often make serious coin while claiming to cure brain cancer with wheatgrass, Shiatsu massage and magnets.

For my part, I'm happy to hitch my wagon to the imperfect but still awesome star of science-based medicine. After all, it wasn't the faith healer who created antibiotics. Or cured polio. Or developed the artificial heart. Prosthetic limbs. Germ theory. Vaccines. Stem cell therapy. Full-face transplants. Birth control. X-rays. The almost endless list of options which aid in prevention, treatment and recovery.

The men and women of medical science have my deepest admiration. They're trained experts in their fields. They often work tirelessly for very little recognition. They endure legions of patients who receive round-the-clock care by human caregivers and then give the credit for their recovery to gods, ghosts and the Virgin Mary. They're on site, on call, on the spot in the moments of our deepest crisis. They're the champions of evidence-based, science-based, reality-based solutions to our most serious health issues. They are the true healers.

And perhaps most importantly, real physicians never, ever ask you to drink your own pee.

CHAPTER 12
Free Long Necks for the Ladies

Body modification. It's our way of telling God, "Hey! You missed a spot."

In the 21st century, body modification has become so commonplace as to be, ironically, invisible. Everywhere we turn, there's a piercing, tattoo or implant of one kind or another.

When I was a kid growing up in corn-fed, Bible-Belt Oklahoma, if someone said they were getting pierced, the natural response was, "Both ears? Or just one?" If it was a guy, the question became, "So how long have you been gay?"

Of course, these accoutrements are nothing new. Piercings have been discovered on 5,000-year-old Egyptian mummies,[154] have long been popular in African tribal culture,[155] and are even referenced in the Old Testament.[156] In the USA, as body modification has edged from subculture to culture, piercings and implants have migrated from the lobes to the lips, eyebrows, noses, nipples, penis and clitoris. Personally, I used to recoil in horror at the idea of genital piercing. After all, I come

---

154 Botchway, C. and Kuc, I. "Tounge Piercing and Associated Tooth Fracture". *Clinical Practice*. Canadian Dental Association. Vol 64, No. 11. 1998. Web.

155 Laderman, Gary and Leon, Luis D. *Religion and American Cultures: An Encyclopedia of Traditions, Diversity, and Popular Expressions*. Volume 1. ABC-CLIO, 2003 (pg. 356-58). Web.

156 *The Holy Bible*. New International Version. Grand Rapids: Zondervan House, 1984. See: Gen 24:47; Ex 32:3; Ex 32:33. Print.

from a region that only knows two kinds of studs (one of them is a horse), and the only fathomable reason someone might have had a 10-gauge, surgical steel barbell funneled through his urethra was that he was in an Iraqi prison.

Cracked.com highlighted genital piercing in a September 2009 article titled, "6 Horrifying Ways to Improve Your Sex Life,"[157] and the author declared that you could emulate the needles used for the average "Prince Albert" by breaking all but one tine from a dinner fork and then stabbing yourself in the crotch.

Of course, body modification exists well beyond the nether regions. Rings, beads, studs and chains proudly adorn human bodies from head to toe. Tattoos (once scandalous in my devoutly religious neighborhood) are now ubiquitous. About 300,000 breast implant surgeries are performed every year.[158] [159] [160] In fact, plastic surgery is a $10 billion a year business, as our "People Magazine" generation cuts, contours, shapes, tucks, stretches, implants, liposuctions and lasers itself into a skin it's more comfortable living in.[161]

I was introduced (as a spectator) to the interesting and occasionally wild world of extreme body modification, most recently in a 2005 film I caught on Netflix called "Modify," which featured real-life characters named The Torture King, Screwfish, Zulu, and Masuimi Max. The flick is informative, fascinating, unflinching and so disturbingly graphic that I spent half the movie curled up on the couch with my hands

157 Hayes, Susan. "6 Horrifying Ways to Improve Your Sex Life". *Cracked.Com*. 24 September 2009. Web.
158 "2013 Plastic Surgery Statistics Report". *American Society of Plastic Surgeons*. 2014. Web.
159 Parker-Pope, Tara. "A Decade of Boosting Breast Size". *New York Times*. 21 March 2011. Web.
160 "The American Society for Aesthetic Plastic Surgery Reports Americans Spent Largest Amount on Cosmetic Surgery Since The Great Recession of 2008". *The American Society for Aesthetic Plastic Surgery*. 20 March 2014. Web.
161 "Cosmetic Surgery: 15 Years of Facts and Figures". *The American Society for Aesthetic Plastic Surgery*. 3 May 2012. Web.

over my loins. (When one guy conducted surgery, sans anesthesia, on his own penis, my dogs thought I was howling at the moon).

Of course, that film highlighted the more extreme cases: branding, scarring, tooth filing, the implantation of horns (yes, horns), corset piercing, hook suspension, tongue splitting, etc, and the poster children for extreme body modification are often sources of fascination for the media and the public.

There's Erik Sprague, "Lizardman," who has transformed himself into a human reptile, complete with a split tongue, five Teflon horns implanted underneath his eyebrows, filed teeth and a green, reptilian pattern covering his entire body.[162]

Julia Gnuse, otherwise known as "The Illustrated Lady," originally used tattoos to cover scarring from a skin condition called porphyria and now holds the Guinness World Record as the most tattooed woman in the world. Her 400-plus tattooed images range from punk bands to Disney characters to favorite retro celebrities. (She actually has Rodney Dangerfield stamped on one of her breasts).[163]

And perhaps the most famous body modifier of all, Dennis Avner of Tonopah, Nevada ("The Catman") was featured on shows like "Ripley's Believe It or Not" and Animal Planet's "Weird, True and Freaky." Why Animal Planet? Because Avner, a Native American, had long been obsessed with his totem animal, the stalking cat. As a result, he underwent extensive tattooing, puffed his face into a feline shape using subdermal implants, shaped his teeth to resemble those of a tiger, sported claw fingernails and even had implants for the wearing of large whiskers. Sadly, after a run of personal troubles, he killed himself

---

162 www.thelizardman.com
163 "Most tattooed woman wins Guinness World Record". *Closer (U.K.)*. 1 January 2010. Web.

in November of 2012.[164]

Some American body modifiers have followed the lead of several groups in Africa, Amazonia and the Pacific Northwest, slotting a clay or wood disk into large, pierced holes in either their upper or lower lips. These alarmingly large lip plates date back to ancient Sudanese and Ethiopian tradition and can reach a diameter of eight inches.[165] (Ain't that a jaw-dropper!) In tribal cultures, they're ornaments, often signifying the rite of passage into adulthood. In the United States, they send a different message, often to prospective employers nervous about any new hire whose lip disk might prevent them from using consonants.

---

164 "Dennis Avner, 'Stalking Cat,' Dead At 54: Body Modification Enthusiast May Have Committed Suicide". *Huffington Post.* 13 November 2012. Web.

165 Turton, David. "Lip-plates and 'the people who take photographs': uneasy encounters between Mursi and tourists in southern Ethiopia". *Anthropology Today.* Vol. 20.3. Pages 3-8, 2004. Web.

Also in the modify-by-disk department, the Kayan women of Burma have a thing about the neck. They don't think they were born with enough of it. As a result, they've decided to strettttttttttttch the limits of the human body to alarming proportions.

Burma isn't exactly known as a tourist mecca. Soldiers and civilians exchange gunfire like you and I exchange phone numbers. And as a result, some Kayan tribes have taken refuge near the Thai border, often using tourism to make their villages and communities self-sufficient. The tourist attractions aren't places or things. They're people. They are Kayan Lahwi: the giraffe women.[166]

You've probably seen internet photos of exotically-dressed females whose abnormally long necks are wrapped in brass coils, their heads pressing out of the top ring like a baby's head emerges from the womb. They move and turn in a slow, pronounced cadence, their heads married to their torsos by what appears to be a large, golden spring, the necks underneath unnaturally elongated and often hidden from the sun for a period of decades. Of course, this brings about the inevitable question of hygiene. How can the neck be properly washed if it's encased in a brass prison? What about zits? Bugs? A really bad itch? And how did those rings get there in the first place? Well, if you'll pardon the expression, allow me to give you a heads-up.

Obviously, this type of body modification doesn't happen overnight, and it doesn't begin at adulthood. In fact, girls are fitted with their first rings around the time that American children start Kindergarten. The neck is slowly yet deliberately stretched under the rings, and over a period of years, smaller coils are replaced with larger ones, and then even larger ones, until the top 1/3 of the body ultimately looks like it was molested by a Slinky.

---

166 Ibuh, Richard. *The Kayans*. Singapore: Partridge Publishing. 2014. Pages 11-12. Print.

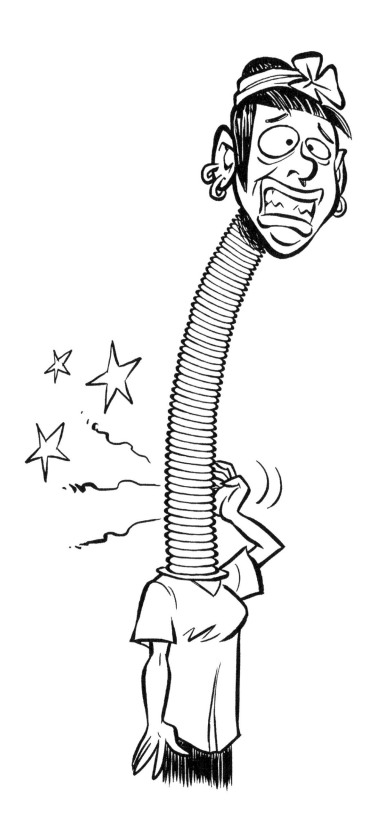

As you can imagine, this places a serious strain on specific parts of the human machine. The collar bone and rib cage are compressed under the weight of the metal collar, and the clavicle becomes deformed. It's a huge commitment that often brings a lot of discomfort and physical stress.[167] (The next time your girlfriend complains about high heels, show her this chapter).

The Kayans are a hugely superstitious people, their religion (Kan Khwan) dating back to the Bronze Age and incorporating icons like dragons and angels. Have you ever joked about someone seeking divination through the examination of chicken bones? The Kayans actually do this.

But religion doesn't seem to drive the whole "giraffe women" practice. No gods or spirits are being honored.[168] There's no theological or patriarchal requirement for the women to parade around like bobbleheads. Some anthropologists think that the unnaturally long necks were defense mechanisms against slavery, as potential masters from other tribes would see them as less physically sound. Others have speculated that the coils simply enhanced the slender female necks that male suitors found attractive. When asked, Kayan women simply assert that the rings are rooted in culture and associated with beauty. It reminds me of the old Steve Martin joke about dating a beautiful woman with no neck, and when he walked into a restaurant with her, every head turned (except hers. She had no neck).

Is the process of becoming a giraffe woman uncomfortable? Absolutely. But while recent years have seen many, especially younger, females remove the coils or reject the process outright, the practice still exists and even thrives in various tribes near the Thai Burma border.

And honestly…I have to give these women props. Surrounded by poverty, oppression and conflict, the Kayan Lahwi have modified

---

167 See Footnote 166.
168 See Footnote 166.

themselves into a unique standard of beauty that brings a feeling of personal worth into their hearts while also bringing financial worth to their homes and towns. And as the rest of us stop, gawk and scratch our heads at these long-necked ladies, they'll continue walking the streets with dignity, smiles, and their heads, literally, held high.

CHAPTER 13
Circus of the Stars

Hollywood isn't exactly known as Credibility Central. We've all suffered through those prime time television moments where talented but flaky movie stars, musicians and pop culture icons attempt to prove that they're not puddle-shallow idiots.

Some classics over the years include Geri Halliwell (Ginger Spice of the Spice Girls) declaring that her mother became a Jehovah's Witness, but she used to be...Spanish.[169] There's Justin Bieber's June 2012 declaration to David Letterman that his rising tattoo count wasn't an attempt to become the "Sixteenth Chapel."[170] In 2002, ear-munching boxer Mike Tyson told ESPN that it was time to "fade into Bolivian."[171] Fox News host Megyn Kelly gained some unwanted notoriety for her 2013 "War on Christmas" rant, which assured a nation of apparently racist children that Santa is a white guy.[172] A personal favorite was the March 1997 appearance by Woody Harrelson on the Barbara Walters' Oscar Special, where he revealed that he refuses to ejaculate during sex

---

169 "Dumb and dumberer: 20 more of the stupidest celebrity quotes ever". *News.Com.AU*. 5 February 2014. Web.

170 Massarella, Linda. "The Sixteenth Chapel?... don't you mean the Sistine? David Letterman gives Justin Bieber a very public history lesson". *Daily Mail (U.K.)* 22 June 2012. Web.

171 Simmons, Bill. "Say 'goodbye' to our little friend". *ESPN*. 11 June 2002. Web.

172 "'Santa just is white ... Jesus was a white man too', says Fox News presenter ." *The Guardian*. 13 December 2013. Web.

so that he can internally recycle his finite supply of sperm.[173]

These people will not be missed at the next MENSA meeting.

I once heard it said that Hollywood earthquakes had lowered the topography of the region to a point where every loose screw just seemed to roll that direction. Perhaps this explains the wispy, weird and often worrying behavior of people like Jenny McCarthy, her background as a Playboy pinup and D-list actor, obviously qualifying her to educate the world on the science of vaccines.[174] Apparently convinced that childhood immunization was responsible for her son's reported autism, her campaign of science-free fear pimping is undoubtedly one of the reasons that the sentence "Do vaccines cause autism?" is a top Google search item.

173 "Barbara Walters Oscars Television Special". *ABC Network*. March 1997. Television.
174 Plait, Phil. "Jenny McCarthy: 'I'm Not "Anti-Vaccine"'". *Slate*. 13 April 2014. Web.

There's Ben Stein, an actor/writer/lawyer/commentator and devout Christian who's on record claiming that the study of science led to the Holocaust, and that evolution is merely some kind of atheistic religion.[175] (That's right, Ben. We dissed Jesus so we could worship biologists.)

And there's Oprah Winfrey, considered by some to be the most influential woman on planet earth, who opened her couch to psychics, new age spiritualists, angel observers, homeopaths, ghost hunters, conspiracy buffs, past life consultants and Dr. Oz. Apparently, the only qualifications to appear as an "expert" on Oprah's show were a discernible pulse, a pretty face and a lab coat. Newsweek even did a story titled, "Why Health Advice on 'Oprah' Could Make You Sick."[176]

"Winfrey Woo Woo" never played well with actual scientists, but daytime audiences lapped it up, and this often-tilted platform provided a grand stage for odd celebrities to do odd things, arguably the most famous instance being Tom Cruise's couch-jumping escapades in May of 2005. He was obviously high on his still-fresh relationship with Katie Holmes, but at that particular time of his life, he was also apparently high on the Church of Scientology. His behavior that year had been almost fanatical. He reportedly set up a Scientology tent on the film set of "War of the Worlds"[177] (which apparently caused director Steven Spielberg much chagrin)[178], and he sat down for a 9-minute video interview earmarked for the church's internal use. (The video leaked in 2008 and went instantly viral.) And of course, Cruise famously choked on his own foot during his 2005 Today

175 Rennie, John. "Ben Stein's Expelled: No Integrity Displayed". *Scientific American.* 9 April 2008. Web.

176 Kosova, Weston. "Why Health Advice on 'Oprah' Could Make You Sick". *Newsweek.* 29 May 2009. Web.

177 J.B., "Tom Cruise Wants to Assist With on-set Scientology" *New York Magazine: Intelligencer.* February 21-28, 2005. Web.

178 "SPIEGEL Interview with Tom Cruise and Steven Spielberg: Actor Tom Cruise Opens Up about his Beliefs in the Church of Scientology". *Spiegel (Germany)* .17 August 2005. Web.

Show sit-down with Matt Lauer, calling the journalist "glib" for daring to suggest that psychiatry might trump Scientology for the purposes of curing mental illness.[179]

Tom Cruise has spent the subsequent years clawing out of the public relations hole he dug for himself, but his hugely public promotion of this relatively unknown organization prompted millions to sit up and ask, "What, exactly, is the Church of Scientology?" Well, thanks to statements by actual Scientologists, the testimonies of ex-Scientologists and the work of a slew of investigative reporters, we now know the answer...and it makes the plot of "Zardoz" look like an Errol Morris documentary. Here's the basic premise:

You aren't a human. Not really. At your core, you're a spirit/soul entity known as a "thetan," the term derived from the Greek letter theta (Θ), which, in Scientology, represents life.[180] Your physical body, a clunky human shell, is merely a temporary place of residence for your thetan, which apparently has hitchhiked on body after body through a kind of reincarnation (called "assumption") for eons.[181]

But as you're not indigenous to earth, how did you get here? Michael Shermer's November 2011 article in Scientific American titled, "The Science Behind Scientology," sums up the Genesis story of Scientology succinctly:

"Around 75 million years ago Xenu, the ruler of a Galactic Confederation of 76 planets, transported billions of his charges in spaceships similar to DC-8 jets to a planet called Teegeeack

179 Silverman, Stephen M. "Tom Cruise Lashes Out at Matt Lauer". *People Magazine*. 24 June 2005. Web.

180 Hubbard, L. Ron. *Dianetics and Scientology Technical Dictionary*. Bridge Publications. June 1975. p. 432. Print.

181 "Does Scientology believe in reincarnation or past lives?". *Scientology Newsroom: The Official Media Resource Center for the Church of Scientology*. 2015. Web.

(Earth). There they were placed in volcanoes and killed by exploding hydrogen bombs, after which their "thetans" (souls) remained to inhabit the bodies of future earthlings, causing humans today great spiritual harm and unhappiness that can be remedied through special techniques involving an Electropsychometer (E-meter) in a process called auditing."

Apparently, thetans are pretty powerful beings, having willed themselves into existence trillions of years ago. They built the universe and once had their run of the place, but having identified so long with this pithy physical realm, they've apparently forgotten their true, deistic nature. This is the "spiritual harm" that Shermer is referring to, and it's the reason that you can no longer manipulate matter and energy like the thetan badass you are and, instead, languish in a kind of spiritual amnesia. Your "reactive mind" (the subconscious part which drives involuntary impulses) needs to be abolished through the revelation and examination of "engrams" (recorded memories) so that you can become "clear" (free of the subconscious).[182]

You're a god smothered by your own skin! If only there was an organization ready to unburden you of all physical constraints and guide you down the path to godhood. Well, never fear, my friends, because the Church of Scientology stands ready to help. Just select your desired method of payment.

For a steadily increasing series of fees, you can submit yourself for a process called "auditing," which is a strange marriage of confession, hypnosis, interrogation and psychotherapy.[183] Defectors like Tory Christman, Claire Headley and others describe the experience as a

---

182 Lewis, Norway James R. *Scientology*. Oxford University Press. 2009. pg. 91-92 Print.
183 Ortega, Tony. "Prepare to Be Audited: Claire Headley Takes Us Through Scientology's 'ARC Straightwire'". *The Underground Bunker*. 7 August 2013. Web.

closed-door guilt-fest driven by leading questions designed to target weakness. Questions are often asked multiple times until the desired answer is given. I picture a scenario like this:

Auditor: "Have you experienced feelings of guilt or shame?"
Subject: "Not really."

Auditor: "Have you experienced feelings of guilt or shame?"
Subject: "I guess it's possible."

Auditor: "Have you experienced feelings of guilt or shame?"

<u>Subject</u>: {lip quivering}

<u>Auditor</u>: "Have you experienced feelings of guilt or shame?"
<u>Subject</u>: "YES! I'M FILLED WITH REMORSE AND SELF-LOATHING!"

<u>Auditor</u>: "That'll be a thousand dollars, please."

During these sessions, the auditor purports to use his/her E-meter like the cops might use a lie detector, monitoring electrical impulses in the skin and interpreting pulses on the graph. But how effective and accurate is an E-meter for the purposes of diagnosing problems? The FDA stepped in decades ago to pose that very question, and U.S. courts now require each device to bear the following disclaimer:[184]

> **The E-Meter is not medically or scientifically useful for the diagnosis, treatment or prevention of any disease. It is not medically or scientifically capable of improving the health or bodily functions of anyone.**

In other words, it's an expensive paperweight. And you're required to pay for it yourself. In fact, according to ex-Scientologist Marc Headley, author of the book "Blown for Good: Behind the Iron Curtain of Scientology," the nifty Mark VIII Super Quantum E-Meter will set you back a cool $5,000.

And...did I mention that these auditing sessions, conducted by people who aren't trained physicians, psychologists or psychiatrists

---

184 United States District Court for the District of Columbia, No. D.C. 1-63. September 29, 1971, as amended by United States Court of Appeals for the District of Columbia, No. 71-2064, March 1, 1973.

and are using devices forbidden for medical diagnosis, can run up to $1000 per hour? In fact, in your pursuit of a state of clarity known as OT III (Operating Thetan Level 3), it's possible that you could fork over hundreds of thousands of dollars, and the stories of ex-Scientologists are rife with examples of multiple mortgages, maxed credit cards, emptied bank accounts and financial ruin. The whole thing is staggering, made even more surreal by the fact that Scientology was originally whipped up by a penny-a-word science fiction writer named L. Ron Hubbard who (according to a first person account by acclaimed author Harlan Ellison and others) once told fellow sci-fi writers that the invention of a new religion would provide an awesome, tax-free revenue stream.[185]

185 Ortega, Tony. "Scientology Mythbusting with Jon Atack: And With Help From Harlan Ellison!". *The Underground Bunker*. 16 February 2013. Web.
    a. Ellison, Harlan. "The Real Harlan Ellison". *Wings*. November-December 1978. Page 32. Web.

A "church" operating as a business and generating tax-free revenue? Stop the presses!

Tom Cruise isn't the only celeb who has lent both name and fame to support the Church of Scientology. John Travolta and Kelly Preston are avid Scientologists. Elisabeth Moss of "Mad Men" is a follower. Kirstie Alley claimed the church helped her beat a cocaine addiction. Laura Prepon of "That 70s Show" and "Orange is the New Black" is a Scientologist. The Huffington Post reported that Fox News host Greta Van Sustren is a Scientologist. Even Nancy Cartwright, the voice of Bart Simpson, is said to be part of the club. But despite the high profile, one investigative reporter (Tony Ortega of "Underground Bunker") estimates that only 25,000 Americans actually belong to the Church of Scientology. That's one person in 12,000.[186]

For some odd reason, the most visible spokespeople for the Church of Scientology often become uncomfortable when asked about the basic tenets of their "faith." Vanilla queries about stress management, balance and bliss are fine, but inject Xenu the Intergalactic Overlord into your line of questioning, and you're likely to see a Scientologist fidget like he's giving birth to a tapeworm. ABC Nightline's Martin Bashir directed the Xenu question to CoS spokesperson Tommy Davis in 2009, and Davis simply walked out of the interview.

He didn't confirm. He didn't deny. He just bolted. Strange behavior for a true believer.

There's little doubt that Scientology hates criticism, and over the

---

186 Ortega, Tony. "Scientologists: How Many Of Them Are There, Anyway?". *The Village Voice*. 4 July 2011. Web.

decades, there have been reports aplenty of pressure, intimidation, coercion and litigation by the organization against its critics. That tide has begun to turn in recent years as the sheer magnitude and volume of criticism has increased, and as a growing number of whistleblowers (including Jenna Miscavige Hill, niece of current CoS leader David Miscavige) tell their stories in the media.

It's a weird, wild, wacky world, this Church of Scientology, with its big names, big claims and big business. But honestly…is the account of Xenu any stranger than the stories of Yahweh or Allah? Is the thetan that different from the eternal soul posited in other churches? Is the auditing session any more outlandish than religious counseling at the corner assembly? Is the high price tag truly different than tithing 10% of one's lifetime income in exchange for blessings? Is the E-meter any more outrageous than a drop of anointing oil, a crucifix or a prayer cloth?

Perhaps this is something we should discuss at length. Just remember that I'm not legitimately qualified, I only take payment in advance, and if you hear the IRS or FDA knocking, tell them we weren't talking about money or medicine. Tell them we were embracing our constitutional religious freedoms. That always seems to do the trick.

CHAPTER 14
Sabbath Mode

The Sabbath. In Judaism, it is known as Shabbat (which is Hebrew for "rest" or "cessation of work"), the seventh day of the week and the Jewish day of rest. It's based on the words of Exodus 31:16: "Wherefore the children of Israel shall keep the Sabbath, to observe the Sabbath, throughout their generations, for a perpetual covenant."

As a protestant-raised, happy-clappy American, I'd always heard that Sunday was the day of rest, which usually meant waking at 8:00 a.m., dressing up, slogging through a morning church sermon, segueing to lunch at a nearby restaurant, scoring a midday nap, mowing the lawn, running some errands, doing a load of laundry, microwaving leftovers, typing an email and falling asleep on the couch midway through a television rerun.

This...was resting, yes?

Actually, compared to observant Jews, I looked like one of those rock-hauling slave kids from "Indiana Jones and the Temple of Doom." At almost every turn, by the strict rules of Jewish law, I had been *working*. To add insult to injury, I'd been violating the Sabbath on the wrong @#$%! day.

It's a complex tradition, but essentially, the Halakha (a collective body of Jewish religious laws) states that the Shabbat is to be observed for 25 hours from Friday evening just a few minutes before sunset through Saturday night.[187] It begins and ends with a blessing, it includes three festive meals, prayer time and singing, and it's allegedly designed to provide an opportunity for spiritual contemplation and family connection.

As God rested on the seventh day after the creation of the world, so his chosen people are charged to "Remember the Sabbath, and keep it holy."
- The 4th Commandment / Exodus 20:8

During the Sabbath, labor is prohibited...specifically "melacha," 39 categories of creative work (referred to in the Torah, relating to the construction of the biblical tabernacle) that exercise dominion over one's environment, including plowing, planting, cooking, combing, shearing, weaving, sewing, slaughtering, tearing, cutting, writing, carrying, kindling, extinguishing, etc.[188]

It's specifically the part about kindling and extinguishing that piqued my interest, as it prevents even the striking of a match or use of a lighter, and that particular prohibition has spawned one of the most bizarre home appliance amenities in history: Sabbath Mode.

For the Sabbath, all cooked foods have to be prepared before the Friday observance begins, and the warming of those foods can't involve re-lighting the oven or stove, as that would constitute an action ("kindling") that is prohibited in the melacha. In the past, families would simply ignite the flame early Friday and keep the oven on a low

187 "Shabbat 101". *MyJewishLearning.Com*. 2015. Web.
188 Eisenberg, Ronald L. "Shabbat's Work Prohibition". *MyJewishLearning.Com*. 2004. Reprinted from *The JPS Guide to Jewish Traditions*, published by the Jewish Publication Society. Web.

burn all weekend, but recent decades have seen manufacturers integrate safety protocols which automatically shut off an appliance after twelve hours. The fire goes out. The oven goes cold. Re-lighting the flame during the Sabbath is forbidden.

Yes, in a world filled with armed conflict, slavery, child abuse, government corruption, disease, disasters, poverty, famine and Kim Kardashian, Yahweh is hugely concerned about preventing Jews from flicking their Bic. Oy vey!

But never fear. Major appliance-makers like Electrolux, Maytag, Kenmore, Whirlpool, GE and others now provide a handy-dandy feature called "Sabbath Mode." Their appliances are rated and certified by organizations like Star-K, a (and I'm totally not kidding) Kosher Certification Agency comprised of rabbis and food technologists which verifies that each unit has achieved "kosher status."[189] [190]

Once the kosher foods are selected, Sabbath Mode ensures that the acts of preparation, warming, cooking and re-heating remain kosher as well. Here's how it works.[191]

When Sabbath Mode is engaged on an oven, no lights, digits, solenoids, fans, icons, tones or displays can be activated. For the most observant Jews, manual temperature adjustments are also forbidden (knob turning = work), so Sabbath Mode can delay the activation of heat/flame many hours after the actual turning of the stove dial. Crank up the temperature knob on Friday, and get warm challah on Saturday.

Congratulations, Jews! You've just outsmarted God.

189 "Taking the Mystery Out of the Certification Process". *Star-K Online*. 2015. Web.
190 "What does Kosher Mean?". *Badatz Igud Rabbonim KIR*. 2015. Web.
191 Ottensoser, Jonah. "The 'Sabbath Mode'". *Star-K Online*. 2015. Web.

KOSHER: From the Hebrew, "Kashrut," meaning <u>suitable</u> and/or <u>pure</u>

Observant Jews believe that "you are what you eat," and the laws of Kashrut comprehensively legislate permitted and forbidden foods. Kosher meat is limited to cattle and game that have "cloven hooves" and "chew the cud." (If a split-hooved animal doesn't chew cud, you don't get to chew the animal.) Meats are to be processed in a specific way that removes certain forbidden fats and veins. Poultry options allow for geese, chickens, ducks and turkeys, with eagles, owls, pelicans, vultures and many other birds off-limits.

Dairy products must come only from kosher animals. Meat and milk may not be combined (per the command of Exodus 23:19). Eggs must come from kosher birds and contain no blood. Acceptable fish must have fins and scales; shellfish is forbidden outright. Fruits and vegetables grown via soil, plants or trees are fine (provided they didn't come from a field combining two seeds), but they must be checked for multi-legged insects that break the kosher code. Wine must be fermented only with certain enzymes and come from a kosher winery that prepares each bottle under strict rabbinical supervision. The list of requirements goes on and on. And it's exhausting.

For the more progressive Jew who is allowed to turn knobs, an organization called (and I'm STILL not kidding) Torah Technologies[192] has developed a contraption called, "The Tweaker," which overrides digital temperature adjustments on modern stoves, shuts off all indicator lights and allows temperature adjustments to be done by hand. What is forbidden digitally is acceptable manually.

In Sabbath Mode, you won't get the benefit of an oven light, because a charged light bulb would involve the closing of an electrical circuit which, of course, takes us back to "kindling." If the light is

---

192 "Shabbos Mode Oven Temperature Adjuster". *Torah Technologies*. 2015. Web.

automatically triggered with the opening of the oven door, you're required to keep the bulb unscrewed for about 25 hours.

Strangely, the other incarnation of "screwing" is perfectly fine during Shabbat, provided it falls inside an ordained marital union.[193] (Does sex not constitute "creative work?") And of course, as per Leviticus 12:3, the participating penis in Jewish sex is foreskin-free, the offending flesh having been removed on the 8th day of the male's life.

In light of my above reference to circumcision, allow me to digress for just a moment to highlight another bizarre Jewish tradition called "metzitzah b'peh,"[194] which translates "oral suction." This alarming

193 Brawer, Naftali and Romain, Jonathan. "Why is sex allowed on Shabbat?". *The Jewish Chronicle Online*. 8 June 2012. Web.
194 JTA. "NY Newborn Contracts Herpes after Metzitzah B'Peh". *Jewish Press.Com*. 3 Febru-

part of the Jewish circumcision ritual has a mohel (circumciser) actually placing his mouth over the freshly cut penis to suck blood from deep within the wound, allegedly preventing infection. To be fair, the majority of observant Jews currently omit this horrifying step, some publicly protest it, and I suppose it's no stranger than other Jewish traditions, like the practice of Kaparot, where a sinful Jew transfers his transgressions into a live chicken by waving it around his head three times before decapitating it. Still, I can't shake the feeling that millions of well-meaning Jewish people have totally gotten punk'd, and God is about to laugh himself right off of the throne.

Now, the staunchly observant Jew who stumbled upon this chapter has almost undoubtedly already started hammering out his protest letter to me and my publisher. "This man is mocking our sacred rituals and traditions! He doesn't understand what Judaism truly is. He has completely missed the point!"

Actually, I totally get the point of ritual, and I'm convinced that cultural traditions and practices can color our lives with beauty, significance and joy. I simply have difficulty understanding why the Most Powerful Being in the Cosmos would care if Grandma Shoshana crocheted a scarf on Saturday. Within 24 hours of the reading of this chapter, 14,000 children will starve to death across the globe, yet Yahweh can't be bothered with them because he's busy commanding his Chosen People to cram their torsos into kitchen appliances?

For my part, I lament any day where we might be forbidden from picking flowers, baking bread, drawing, painting, stringing a guitar, grinding coffee, tying shoelaces, hanging a birdhouse, skating, driving, shooting hoops, dog walking, playing cards, flying kites, tossing

ary 2014. Web.
    a.   Rose, Joel. "New York, Orthodox Jews Clash Over Circumcision". *National Public Radio*. 3 December 2012 6:00pm ET. Web.

Frisbees, swimming, writing letters to friends and family, fully acting, interacting and creating until our hearts are content. This is the good stuff…the marrow of life, and it often requires a hands-on approach.

Getting your tallit in a twist because interpreters of an anonymously-written, Iron Age text have declared it spiritually illegal to light an oven on the Sabbath?

C'mon…that's just sad.

CHAPTER 15
Can You Put Me Up For The Night?

I grew up in a protestant Christian church, and its franchise player was Jesus. From my earliest years in vacation bible school, the stories of Christ's birth, miracles, death and resurrection framed my spiritual training.

Much was made of the crucifixion, as that act of divine sacrifice was said to atone for the fact that my great, great, great, great, great, great, great, great, great, great grandfather nibbled on the wrong food. For this heinous act in the Garden of Eden, all of Adam's descendants received a death sentence, the Governor's pardon coming in the form of a god-man, a pissed-off mob, a cross, three nails and a spear.

Death by crucifixion has always been a nasty affair, dating back to ancient Persia, Carthage, Macedonia and Rome and designed to instill serious fear and allegiance in the heart of anyone who witnessed it. In fact, the English word "excruciating" is derived from the Latin terms "excruciare" and "cruciare," meaning "torment" and "crucify," respectively.[195]

---

195 "Excruciating, n.". *Dictionary.com*. 2015. Web.

Throughout history, there have been many variations on this macabre practice. Some convicts were simply roped to the wooden beams, while others were nailed. Cross shapes varied from a "T" shape to an "X" or "Y." It wasn't unheard of to be crucified upside down or leaning at some odd angle. Legs were often broken, putting the painful wrist spikes to full effect and hastening death. The ordeal could last mere hours, or it could drag on for days. Death resulted from any combination of shock, heart failure, dehydration, asphyxia, infection and more. Just grisly stuff.[196] [197]

The emperor, Constantine, abolished crucifixion in the Roman empire in 337 CE as an act of reverence to his savior, Jesus Christ.[198]

It almost seems odd that I was so exposed to Jesus' crucifixion story in my formative years. Parents shield their young children from restricted films depicting gunshot wounds, knife wounds, physical abuse and excessive gore, but they're perfectly willing to allow Sunday School lessons featuring full-color drawings of a shredded Jewish guy heaving on a cross with pikes driven through his limbs.

Granted, for the youngest eyes, child-targeted material about Jesus' death is relatively benign, depicting a scant amount of blood with Christ's flesh remarkably unscathed. As children grow, so does the intensity of the imagery presented to them, moving from vanilla Sunday School illustrations to more intense Passion Play reenactments and ultimately culminating in the equivalent of Mel Gibson's "The Passion of the Christ," two hours of crimson-spattered torture porn mostly designed to shock an audience into dropping to its knees. *Jesus went through all of this for you*! (cue altar call)

---

196 "Crucifixion, Capital Punishment". *Encyclopedia Britannica*. Encyclopedia Britannica, 9 March 2015. Web.

197 Retief, F.P. and Cilliers, L. "The history and pathology of crucifixion". *South African Medical Journal*. Vol 93(12). December 2003. Pages 938-41. Print.

198 See Footnote 196.

The ultimate point is that Christ sacrificed himself on our behalf, this selfless and divine act providing inspiration for countless hymns sung down through the ages:

> *Jesus paid it all.*
> *All to Him I owe.*
> *Sin had left a crimson stain.*
> *He washed it white as snow.*

1 Peter 1:3 declares, "Praise be to the God and Father of our Lord Jesus Christ! In his great mercy he has given us new birth into a living hope through the resurrection of Jesus Christ from the dead."

Indeed, according to Christian scripture and tradition, Jesus died on a cross so we don't have to.

Well, there are villages in the Philippines that apparently never got that memo, and every Easter, to commemorate Christ's sacrifice, several of the faithful insist on beating themselves to a pulp and having themselves tacked up like a five dollar crucifix.

Thousands of tourists annually flock to the Pampanga province to watch this unique Easter spectacle, the Good Friday festivities beginning with a troupe of male and female penitents slogging through the village streets carrying homemade whips and wailing in agony as they flagellate themselves bloody. Others drag heavy wooden crosses, imitating Jesus' act from John 19:17. It's a long, loud, miserable push toward the grand finale, the actual, literal crucifixion of willing volunteers who are convinced that pinning themselves to crosses will atone for sin, bring about good luck, produce miracles for the afflicted and show gratitude to God.

(If I may digress, I'm reminded of that internet meme that shows some poor bastard hanging on a cross, and the caption reads, "Not going anywhere? Try a Snickers!")

Ruben Enaje of the San Pedro Cutud Village told the Associated Press that his 2014 crucifixion was his 28th.[199] It boggles the mind. On almost thirty separate occasions, this guy showed up to the party, willingly pummeled himself with a cat of nine tails, grabbed some guys trussed up like Roman soldiers and asked them to essentially staple him to a board.

To (literally) amplify this divine comedy, Enaje was fitted with a wireless microphone,[200] just in case the back section of gawking rubberneckers wasn't able to hear his screams.

---

199 Favila, Aaron. "In The Philippines, Observers Perform Crucifixion Reenactment In Good Friday Ritual". *Huffington Post.* 18 April 2014. Web.

200 Favila, Aaron. "Filipino Crucifixion Reenactment On Good Friday Draws Penitents And Onlookers". *Huffington Post.* 29 March 2013. Web.

For all of the crucifixees (is that even a word?), the routine goes something like this:

1.) Flog yourself silly.
2.) Get nailed to a cross.
3.) Hang under the hot sun for a few minutes.
4.) Have yourself pried loose.
5.) Get hauled off to receive first aid.

Those brave (aka: stupid) enough to participate in this tradition of self-crucifixion are encouraged, for reasons of safety and hygiene, to get advance tetanus shots and only use sterilized nails. After all, when having cold steel driven through healthy flesh for the purpose of ritual torture, it's important to exercise cleanliness and prevent any nasty infections.

This dark little dance has become such a popular tourist attraction that area gift shops actually sell crucifixion nails (!) to passing patrons. Yep. Just as the Roman executions of old were a carnival of morbid fascination and commerce, 21st century crucifixion experiences just aren't complete until you've scored some killer cell phone video and a sack of commemorative spikes for the kids.[201]

Of course, in light of the Christ story, all of this seems even more

---

201 Regala, Franco G. "Pampanga braces for pilgrims, tourists at 4 crucifixion sites today". *Manila Bulletin*. 18 April 2014. Web.

ludicrous, as the atonement made 2,000 years ago is supposed to have rendered all of this contemporary suffering moot and pointless. It's like a child rescued from a burning building insisting that he barge back into the inferno because he felt his flesh hadn't been properly singed.

If the Christian God exists, would this really be his desired method for commemorating Holy Week and remembering the Easter story? Or does he spend every Easter weekend peering down onto a Philippine village with a "You've gotta be shittin' me" look on his face, baffled that so many would consider the sacrifice of a god *simply not enough* to cover things.

If I was Jesus, I guarantee you that I'd immediately part the curtain of the sky, descend in a burst of golden light onto the Pampanga town square and declare (in my James Earl Jones voice) that "ALL SELF-CRUCIFIXIONS MUST CEASE FORTHWITH." I'd clear the air, save dozens of self-mutilators another three decades of pain, and miraculously heal everyone's scars (just because I could) before rocketing back to my gilded throne, my pearly gates and my water-to-wine mini bar.

After all, Easter is a cause for celebration, and Jesus never misses an opportunity to get good and hammered.

CHAPTER 16
Wag The Dog

This one sets my blood to boiling, and I have a hunch you'll be my rage buddy by the end of this chapter.

I consider myself a compassionate person, a teddy bear, an "I'd like to buy the world a Coke" humanist who blanches at the barrage of person-against-person mistreatment that fills 90% of the typical CNN news day. And I'm guessing that you're much like me, genuinely grieved every time a fellow human being is injured, accosted, harmed or maligned by another. With each instance of abuse or neglect, our innate sense of goodness and justice stresses under the strain, and we say to each other, "That's just terrible."

But here's the thing. My spark of outrage goes nuclear whenever I hear about the abuse of an animal. It's difficult to describe really, and I know my admittedly emotional response is disproportional in the light of so much human tragedy in this world. Someone tells me about a guy clubbing his buddy with a baseball bat, and I reply, "Geez, that's awful." Someone tells me about a guy clubbing his golden retriever with a baseball bat, and my eyes flare, my skin turns red, my face clenches like a fist, and I suddenly consider becoming a supporter of the death penalty.

I had this very reaction when I was told about a tradition that is still being practiced in rural Bulgaria. It's called "Trichane," which translates "dog spinning." And it's just as bad as it sounds.

For hundreds of years, residents of a town called Brodilovo have sought to "cleanse" the community of evil, ward off rabies and bring about fertility to the land and its people, and their method of doing so involves a body of water, a rope and a canine. The practice has a long history in Bulgaria,[202] and here's how it works:

The townspeople gather around a custom-built "spinning" apparatus which has been erected over a river. Several residents willingly bring their own dogs just for the occasion. A rope descending from a high perch is tied around the animal's waist, and the dog is then turned repeatedly to coil the rope. Once the cord is twisted to its limits, the dog is released to spin and flail wildly as the rope unwinds, until the poor animal finally disconnects and splashes into the creek.

The locals call this harmless, as they say the actual spinning only takes (an eternal) 15-20 seconds, and because the ultimate immersion in water is not unlike merely giving the dog a bath. I shit you not. This is their defense of Trichane.

The saddest part is that many dogs are so dizzy and disoriented by the time they hit the water that they drown.

When the news media outside of Bulgaria finally caught wind of this barbaric practice, animal rights groups descended upon the dog spinners with justifiable outrage. In the light/heat of those protests, dog spinning was stopped in 2005 before ultimately being reinstated six

---

202   Smith, Graham. "Exposed: The cruel dog-spinning ritual to 'ward off rabies' that is STILL being practised Bulgaria". *Daily Mail (U.K.)*. 28 February 2012. Web.
    a.   Coren Ph.D., Stanley. "Religious Rituals and Dog Abuse: The Bizaare Case of Dog Spinning". *Psychology Today*. 15 May 2012. Web.

years later. According to a 2011 statement given by Petko Arnaudov, the mayor of Brodilovo, the international community has "misinterpreted" what Trichane is all about, and in the wake of a recent plague on the local farming community, spinning dogs is a vital and really, really necessary good luck charm. It also purges evil and promotes fertility.

You cannot make this stuff up.

In the wake of further protests, it's been said that Brodilovo's residents have "softened" the ritual a bit, foregoing the rope altogether and merely tossing the dog into the water. Why the gods, spirits or whatever would require a soaking wet dog to spill out their blessings is beyond me. (*"You know, our corn harvest has been rather pithy this season. Bring me some rope and a puppy!"*)

It's tragic that, so often, the helpless and innocent have to pay the price for the collective insanity of humankind, yet these examples exist across the globe. Here are just a few gems.

In the province of Manganeses de la Polvorosa of Zamora, Spain, villagers used to honor their patron Saint Vincent every 4th Sunday in June by dragging a live goat to the top of a church and then flinging it from the roof. An enthusiastic crowd would be waiting below with a stretched sheet to catch the animal before parading it through the streets. Occasionally, the goat wouldn't survive the fall, but alive or dead, its descent from the belfry would signal the commencement of a grand fiesta. The custom was banned in 1992. Unfortunately, the ban has largely been ignored over the subsequent years. I was encouraged to read that practice was recently toned down (they merely lowered the goat down on a rope...woo!),[203] and that the 2014 celebration involved a toy plush goat instead of a live one.[204]

Goats have gotten short shrift since Old Testament times (and likely before), when, according to Leviticus 16, Mosiac law declared that two goats were required for the payment of sins on the Day of Atonement. Both animals would be presented at the Tabernacle. One would be slaughtered/sacrificed on the altar, and the other goat (carrying the sins of the people) would be sent off to "escape" into the wilderness, where it would presumably die of starvation or be killed by a predator. (Incidentally, this reference to the "escape goat" is where we get the term, "scapegoat.")[205]

In annual festivals throughout India, they're not dropping goats. They're tossing babies. Temples in Maharashtra, Solapur, Indi and

203 Juniquera, Natalia. "Spain's celebrations of cruelty". *El Pais (Spain)*. 24 September 2014. Web.
204 "Spaniards Won't Throw Goat". *CBS News*. 11 January 2000. Web.
205 Brasch, R. and Brasch, L. *How Did It Begin The Origins of our Curious Customs and Superstitions*. New York: MJF Books. 2006. Page 173. Print.

other villages seek to ensure the good health, good luck, long life and success of their youngest children by dragging helpless infants (two years and younger) to the tops of temples and towers, hoisting them over ledges and dropping the terrified tykes 50 feet to be caught on outstretched cloths below.[206] The videos of these ceremonies, easily found on YouTube, are horrifying. Human rights organizations agree, but this dangerous practice continues as a protected custom (and serves as another example of why "We've always done it this way" is a ridiculous rationalization of abusive behavior).

At least human *adults* bear the brunt of the blows in Tamil Nadu during the Adi festival of Sri Mahalakshmiamman Temple. (No, I can't pronounce it either.) In a practice said to be centuries old, hundreds of men, women and children converge at this small state in southern India to petition the gods for good luck, good health and success, and they do this by asking a chief priest to smash a coconut onto their heads.

A holy man begins the ceremony by standing on a bed of nails placed behind a sitting row of the community's seven elders, initiating each

---

206 "Indian Baby-Dropping Ritual At Baba Umer Durga, A Local Shrine, Is Unreal". *Huffington Post*. 25 February 2014. Web.
    a.   "Villagers throw babies from temple roof". *CNN*. 1 May 2008. Web.

one of them with a coconut crack to the noggin. Then, with his assistants in tow (one to hold the heads of the crushees, the other to supply fresh coconut ammo), he walks a long, long line of seated devotees who wait their turn with increasing anticipation, possibly lamenting that the gods don't smile upon helmets.

One by one, with alarming violence, hard coconut meets hard skull, these acts of "blessing" often requiring medical treatment by attending paramedics. Many of the injured skip the ambulance ride and simply sprinkle their bleeding craniums with "vibhuthi" (sacred ash). Some keep the shattered coconut pieces as offerings.[207] (Apparently, some protestors have spoken out against this bloody game of Whack-A-Mole, but the faithful just won't get it through their thick skulls.)

There's the Land Diving ritual of Vanuato, where men attempt to increase the coming harvest (and risk broken necks) by leaping from wooden towers, their bungee cords consisting of two vines tied around the ankles.[208] The fire-walkers of Malaysia walk on burning embers to purge themselves of evil spirits. Evil is warded off in Phuket, Thailand as willing participants ram knives, swords and spears through their own faces.[209] (Side note: They're all vegetarians, which is strange for people so adept at slicing meat.) At the Catholic festival of Corpus Christi in northern Spain, men dressed up as the devil jump over babies to proclaim their victory over Satan.[210] And so on.

This seemingly endless list of ridiculous rites and rituals becomes a showcase for absurdity, the common denominator for these circus

207 "Coconut-breaking ritual at temple in Karur village incident-free". *The Hindu (India)*. 5 August 2007. Web.
   a.   "Priests Crack Coconuts on Devotees' Heads". *National Geographic News*. 6 August 2009.
208 Lee, Mike. "Land Divers of Vanuata". *ABC News*. 25 July 2013. Web.
209 "Bloody ritual at Thai festival". *CBS News*. 29 September 2014. Web.
210 Becker, Olivia. "Spain Held Its Annual Devil Baby Jumping Festival". *Vice News*. 23 June 2014. Web.

acts being the attempt to cull favor from an unseen hand. Because we're convinced that goodness and fortune must come from an invisible "other," we spin the canine, we drop the goat, we toss the baby, we smash the holy coconuts, we present the sacrifice, and we dance a comical choreography of strict ritual and pain. We're choking on the dense smoke of our own offerings as these traditions drive our non-sensical behavior.

Indeed, the tail is wagging the dog.

Perhaps, one day, the dog-twirling villagers of Brodilovo (and their ilk) will snap out of their superstitious funk and begin to see ridiculous acts of cruelty through the eyes of reason. They'll not see sacred tradition. They'll see insanity. And it will make their heads spin.

CHAPTER 17
The Order, the Doctrine and the Dude

As a casual student of faith and philosophy and a lifelong fan of Star Wars, I recently became aware of a Jedi order far beyond the multiplexes and video stores.

For some, the Jedi are merely fictional heroes from a long time ago and a galaxy far, far away. But for others, Jedi is a way of life, a code of conduct, a higher calling. Hence, a series of sci-fi movies has spawned a very real (and non-theistic) religion, branching into several "denominations," that charges each member to be a guardian of peace, honor and justice here on 21st century planet earth:

Jediism.

Before we get into the details, let me make something perfectly clear. When I refer to "Star Wars," in no way am I referencing the cretinous, pathetic, awful, sad, incompetently-produced, soul-sucking piles of bantha butter that are the prequel films. With all due respect to George Lucas, I've chosen to believe that he died peacefully in his sleep back in 1997, and as a result, he was never allowed to foist upon the public blasphemies like space taxes, Jar Jar, battle droids, Jake Lloyd, midi-chlorians, geisha queens, prophecies, digital Yodas, lightsaber orgies, iguana horses, younglings, the murder-by-dismemberment of younglings, clones, a flying R2D2, Mace Windu and any other character whose name sounds like a brand of yo-yo.

No, the prequel films never happened, and as such, the fond recollections of the Star Wars from our childhood remain safe and unspoiled. (Come to think of it, let's move that RIP date back to 1984, which will prevent another ill-fated George Lucas production, "Howard the Duck." You can thank me later.)

In the classic Star Wars trilogy, a Jedi wasn't a character so much as an aspiration, a higher goal to be attained, and millions of wide-eyed kids ached to trade places with Luke Skywalker as he abandoned his bland, humdrum existence on Tatooine for a life of challenge, discovery, adventure and heroism. Actually, adults connected with this fantasy as much as the children, as anyone who has ever felt trapped in an "Office Space" hell of repetition, paperwork and skull-numbing monotony has dreamed of breaking out and putting a bland, boring existence in the rear view mirror.

According to the Star Wars "Wookieepedia" page, The Jedi Order "was an ancient monastic peacekeeping organization unified by its belief and observance of the Force, specifically the light side. The Jedi were the guardians of peace and justice in the Galactic Republic."[211]

Jediism, surprisingly, doesn't hold a strict allegiance to the holy canon of Star Wars, nor is it merely a churchy fan club. These folks don't just sit around arguing whether or not the Millennium Falcon could actually make the Kessel Run in less than twelve parsecs (GEEK HINT: It can't, because parsecs are units of light-travel distance and not units of time), or the specs of moisture vaporators, or why stormtrooper armor appeared

---

211 "Jedi Order". *Wookieepedia*. *Wikipedia*. 2015. Web.

to be made out of rice paper, or whether they'd rather be trapped on a deserted island with hair-bun Leia, snowsuit Leia or slave girl Leia.

Those topics are for fan clubs. This is the serious business of Jediism. And one of the most prominent branches (denominations?) of Jediism is The Temple of the Jedi Order.

The Temple of the Jedi Order (TOTJO) has no deity, no holy book, no physical building, no significant infrastructure, and it claims no superiority or mutual exclusivity regarding other religious beliefs. Where the Lucasfilm Jedi spent years honing themselves to achieve physical and spiritual transcendence, the TOTJO candidates need only a few seconds to register a free account and pledge allegiance to the temple Doctrine.[212] The Temple of the Jedi Order believe:

- In the Force, and in the inherent worth of all life within it.

- In the sanctity of the human person. We oppose the use of torture and cruel or unusual punishment, including the death penalty.

- In a society governed by laws grounded in reason and compassion, not in fear or prejudice.

- In a society that does not discriminate on the basis of sexual orientation or circumstances of birth such as gender, ethnicity and national origin.

- In the ethic of reciprocity, and how moral concepts are not absolute but vary by culture, religion, and over time.

- In the positive influence of spiritual growth and awareness on society.

---

212 "Doctrine of the Order". *Temple of the Jedi Order.* 2015. Web.

- In the importance of freedom of conscience and self-determination within religious, political and other structures.

- In the separation of religion and government and the freedoms of speech, association, and expression.

Outside of occasional references to things like "spiritual awareness," the Temple of the Jedi Order actually promotes rather humanistic philosophies: Govern with reason and compassion. Oppose cruelty and injustice. Fight discrimination and bigotry. Keep the church and state boundary intact. Live a moral life. Develop knowledge and wisdom. Good stuff!

But then suddenly, TOTJO slides into weird, vague mysticism, with a head-scratcher of an Orthodox Code:[213]

- There is no Emotion; There is Peace.

- There is no Ignorance; There is Knowledge.

- There is no Passion; There is Serenity.

- There is no Chaos; There is Harmony.

- There is no Death; There is the Force.

"The 16 Teachings" tout the merits of tuning one's mind, of achieving clarity through meditation and contemplation, of remaining fluid and adaptable, of being patient, of having integrity, of demonstrating love and compassion, of serving humanity, and ultimately achieving "eternal life through the Force," whatever that means. The "21 Maxims" promote things like loyalty, focus, harmony, discipline, pure

---

213 See Footnote 212.

motive, prowess and nobility, these attributes wrapped in the "faith of the Force."

Honestly, it's like George Lucas, Christopher Hitchens, Gandhi and Deepak Choprah met at a bar, got completely schnockered and scribbled this stuff on a napkin.

The Temple of the Jedi Order offers an Initiate Program which touches on myths, takes a comparative look at world religions (although the Force really needs to tell these folks that atheism isn't a religion), and provides an in-depth study of the TOTJO creed and code. Its site provides sermons with titles like "Darkness," "A Basket of Eggs -- A Story of Us," "Mental Healing," and "The Root of all Fear," each message written by a licensed and ordained Jedi minister.

Jedi ministers are actual clergy, their licenses recognized in all 50 U.S. states. They can officiate at weddings and conduct religious ceremonies. Ordination requires actual clerical training through the Jedi seminary and a vote by an actual Jedi Council. Upon approval, the candidate becomes an official "Minister of the Force," which undoubtedly looks *totally* badass on a business card.

It must be said that The Temple of the Jedi Order is not the only organization of its kind. JediChurch.org also offers free membership (with the optional $20 certificate bearing your name). Other options for the aspiring apprentice include The Jedi Website, the Jedi Academy Online, Order of the Jedi and Temple of the Jedi Force, the doctrines of each being a similar mash-up of the existential, the mystic and the humanistic.

As I understand it, there has been frustration within Jediism that it isn't taken seriously by the public, because it's a religion based on an obviously fictitious and fantastical story. I find the rejection of Jediism rather hypocritical, especially when you take a comparative look at Jediism against mainstream faiths like Christianity, Islam and Hinduism. After all, Jediism doesn't assert that penguins walked thousands of miles to board a boat built by a 600-year-old man in the desert (Genesis 7:8), or that humans were created from a clot of blood transformed out of sperm harvested between the backbone and ribs (Sura 96:1-2, Qur'an 86:7), or that one can wish upon a magic cow (Bhagavad Gita 3:10).

If it's all relative, Jediism comes off as rather pedestrian, don't you think? And in case you were curious, it's not the only such group with roots in contemporary film. Those who prefer Shatner over Skywalker can browse the web to discover a number of Star Trek-related worldviews, including humanism, Vulcan philosophy, and the warrior traditions of the Klingons. On a related note, Christian fans of Star Trek will be delighted to hear that the biblical book of Psalms has been translated into Klingon ("ghurtaH ghaH the loD 'Iv ta'be' yIt Daq the qeS vo' the mIgh" - Psalms 1:1). Of course, as Star Trek was conceived by the late Gene Roddenberry, an atheist with only disdain for Christianity, this particular melding of fictions probably has him rolling in his grave.

Fans of the Coen brothers' classic, "The Big Lebowski," can abide in the relaxing Zen of Dudeism, a mishmash of Taoism and Epicureanism which promotes a "go with the flow" mentality in all things. In our highly materialistic world where a lack of physical wealth and possessions can cause some to feel inferior, Dudeists instead embrace simple pleasures like reading a book, chilling with friends, enjoying a favorite food, walking the dog, taking a bath, lounging in comfortable clothes, and, of course, bowling.

A modest, stress-free, pain-free life is a Dudeist heaven, and while Dudeism sounds like merely an inside joke for Lebowski aficionados, it's apparently a *thing*, with 250,000 Dudeist priests ordained into The Church of the Latter Day Dude.[214] Upon receiving this information, I immediately logged onto dudeism.com and had myself ordained. It didn't cost me a dime, and the site only required that I take a vow and affirmation:

> **DUDEIST VOW**: I vow to uphold the principles of Dudeism; To just take it easy, to be *dude* (easygoing) to everyone I meet, and to keep my mind limber.

> **AFFIRMATION**: I affirm that this ordination is for me and not for someone else, or my dog or whatever.

That was it. Now, like the Jedi Ministers of the Force , I am clergy.

Basking in my post-ordination glow, I pondered having myself renamed...like the Pope. I also considered marching into the bedroom and insisting that my wife address me as Father, but that just seemed creepy. What moniker fit my newly elevated clerical status? Pastor? Minister? Bishop? Rabbi? Dean? Deacon? And then, suddenly, I

---

214 "The Way of the Dude". *Nightline*. ABC. Retrieved 20 September 2012.

realized that I had been complicating the simple. Two minutes as a Dudeist, and I was already violating one of my church's basic tenets. (I could almost hear Walter Sobchak in my skull, yelling "Over the line!")

To regain my bliss, I browsed the website for awhile, and I was surprised to see Jesus Christ listed among the Great Dudes in History (alongside Lao Tzu, Snoopy and Jerry Garcia). Their brief biography on Christ reveals that, although he was born Jewish, he converted to Dudeism because the Romans and Pharisees were "fucking fascists." This makes sense, as they're honoring the happy, hippie "let us love one another" Jesus and not the rug-pisser Jesus that created Hell. (That second Jesus is so very un-Dude.)

Ultimately, from the Doctrine of the Jedi Order to the Abide Guide of the Dudeists, we see people creatively organizing to promote health, happiness and humanism, decorating their philosophies with their favorite films (and the occasional sprinkle of woo), transforming bland, boring clerical clothing into hooded robes and pajama bottoms, and spreading a message we might all embrace:

Promote equality. Celebrate diversity. Help a stranger. Make a friend. Enjoy the little things. And, above all...abide.

Can I get an Amen?

CHAPTER 18
Running with the Devil

Roll the devil's dice, pay a heavy price.

This was a sobering warning to those of us who had ever toyed with the idea of playing Dungeons & Dragons, the hugely popular, dice-based fantasy game played by our heathen friends in their bedrooms, back rooms and basements. These nerdy rogues would slip quietly away from polite society, don their black fingernail polish, fire up the Ozzy albums and delve into the dark magic of D&D, climbing ladders, advancing levels, enhancing armor and casting the spells of witches and wizards upon each other, even after being warned that that they were playing with literal fire.

Hellfire.

This ominous threat was drilled into thousands of Bible Belt kids in the 1980s and early 1990s, a decade-long season of hysteria now affectionately known as the "Satanic Panic."[215] Children were told that those who played Dungeons & Dragons often found themselves the victims of malice and malady. They'd lose their identities as demons possessed their physical bodies. They'd be taunted and haunted by malevolent spirits. They might ultimately kill themselves...or kill others.

---

215 "Satanic Panic". *Rational Wiki. Wikipedia.* 2015. Web.

One didn't simply pretend to be a mage imbued with dark supernatural power without opening the actual portals of dark supernatural power. The devil was already at the heart's door trying to pick the lock. D&D gave him an engraved invitation, made him the guest of honor, and transformed the whole party into a Satanic cult ritual.

In those early years, the world oozed the dark ectoplasm of evil, and the problem went far beyond Dungeons & Dragons. The "panic" of that decade was so intense, I'm surprised my sisters and I weren't escorted to school by a cadre of armed priests. Christian leaders like Jerry Falwell, Pat Robertson, Hal Lindsey, Bob Larson and a host of corner-church preachers wailed about a generation teetering on the razor's edge between Heaven and Hell. Parents, pastors and politicians told horror stories about Satan-worshipping families hiding their virgin-sacrificing, child-abusing, blood-drinking ways behind a benign, Brady Bunch facade designed to lure in the naive and unsuspecting. Beelzebub had infiltrated communities, government offices, corporations, even law enforcement. Pop culture was loaded with devilry. The deeply religious wrapped a long roll of crime scene tape around the devil's holiday, Halloween. And a generation shuddered with fear and dread at any mention of that diabolical den of damnation, the Church of Satan.

Hang with me here, because there's a plot twist coming that could spin Jerry Falwell out of his coffin. But first, I'd like to put some detail on my portrait of the devil's decade.

Back before the era of digital music, we played albums. Yes, those clunky, clumsy, flimsy, scratched, warped, chipped and absolutely awesome vinyl disks bearing only a dozen songs each and requiring a machine the size of a microwave oven to play them. (No, I'm not one of those geezer snobs yearning for yesteryear, but there was a charm to the classic vinyl album that does make my generation a bit misty.) And 99.999% of my generation played those albums in the method that was intended: clockwise!

However, holy whistleblowers warned of a phenomenon called "backmasking,"[216] where Satanic messages (often voiced by the Dark Lord himself) were embedded within the grooves of records and only revealed when songs were played *in reverse*. When I first heard this astonishing news at the age of 14, I was riveted. I then proceeded to ruin a dozen phonograph needles as I manually spun every album I owned backward in an obsessive hunt for hidden words, phrases, chants or commands. Suddenly, I felt surrounded by sinister voices saying things like, "shhhrrvv shattin," which was obviously an embedded prompt to "serve Satan." Every few moments of reverse-spinning revealed another smoking gun and more proof that the devil had infiltrated

---

216 "Backward Satanic Messages". *The Skeptic's Dictionary*. Edited by Carroll, Robert Todd. 12 September 2014. Web.

our favorite bands and radio singles. Queen, the Eagles, Deep Purple, ELO, Styx, Zepplin and so many others weren't just musical groups. They were ambassadors of supernatural darkness and death.

Who knew?

Fueling these fearful flames were prophets of doom like John Todd,[217] a popular evangelist in the 1970s who claimed to have been born into a family of witches and groomed for the Illuminati before making his escape. Todd was featured in a number of illustrated tracts produced by Jack Chick (those religious comics are widely known as Chick tracts) warning of the devil in D&D, rock music and Ouija boards.[218]

Investigations into John Todd's professed history resulted in strong evidence that he was lying his ass off.

Another hugely popular product of the Satanic Panic was Mike Warnke, a former Satanist high priest who accepted Christ, toured the world as a Christian comedian and built a 7-figure ministry on stories of his sordid, Satanic past. He published a best-selling autobiography titled, "The Satan Seller," which detailed Warnke's participation in Satanic rituals, the summoning of demons and the casting of spells.

Investigations into Mike Warnke's professed history resulted in over-whelming evidence that he was lying his ass off.[219]

Christians were presented with books and documentary films like 1986's, "Turmoil in the Toybox," with author/host Phil Phillips

217 Elliott, S.M. "John Todd, 'Former Witch' and 'Illuminati Insider'". *Speak of the Devil (blog)*. 8 April 2011. Web.
    a.   "John Todd". *Rational Wiki. Wikipedia*. 2015. Web.
218 See Footnote 215.
219 Hertenstein, Mike and Trott, Jon. *Selling Satan: The Evangelical Media and the Mike Warnke Scandal*. Chicago: Cornerstone Press. July 1993. Print.

charging that the devil's doings echoed far beyond the grooves of pop, rock and metal albums and spilled into the not-so-harmless playthings that unsuspecting parents were approving for their children. He-Man claimed to be "Master of the Universe" and was therefore directly attempting to usurp God on the throne. G.I. Joe was an agent of "necromology" and enacted the spells of witches. Star Wars fans were horrified to learn that Obi Wan Kenobi represented a special form of witchcraft ("Obi witchcraft"), and that Yoda was the "three-fingered, three-toed beast" representing allegiance to Satan. Smurfs were depicted as blue with black lips, representative of "dead creatures." Other totems of evil included the Care Bears, Mighty Mouse and My Little Pony.

Investigations into Phil Phillips' history resulted in overwhelming evidence that he was either 1) lying his ass off or 2) out of his fucking mind.

During the height of the Satanic Panic, otherwise rational people were rifling through their bookshelves, music collections and toyboxes for anything bearing hooves, horns, flames, pentagrams, pyramids, inverted crosses, skulls, altars, blood, magic wands, black cloaks, talismans, hidden codes, pagan symbols and the number 6, tossing these fiendish fads into actual bonfires (often at Christian church services). The evil had to be rooted out and excised! A generation was at stake!

This was the witch hunt of the 20th century. And the ultimate witches' coven was the devil's earthly fraternity: the Church of Satan.

Church. Of. Satan. Say those three words aloud to almost any protestant Christian, and you're likely to see the blood drain from his face. Say you're a *member* of the Church of Satan, and watch him lurch backward like you're vomiting fire ants. Ask him what he knows about the Church of Satan, and I'd wager you'll hear the same answer I would have given during the height of the Satanic Panic:

1.) It's a cult.

2.) Its members worship Satan.

3.) It sacrifices animals and babies to the devil.

4.) It's *scary*.

Well, *obviously*, these points are correct. It's the Church of Satan. This is what they do. This is what we've always been told. But let's take a moment and do something audacious. Let's do some homework on the CoS and find out what those evil necromancers are really all about. And to do so, we must start with its founder, a fiendish-looking rogue named Anton LaVey.

Born in 1930, Anton Szandor Lavey (whose birth name was actually Howard) was a high-school dropout turned circus performer who often used his skills as an organist in nightclubs. Theatrical and provocative, he gave performances as a "paranormal" researcher and, in short order, became a kind of San Francisco celebrity. LaVey was fascinated by unusual and bizarre things, especially the occult and the supernatural, but (and this is important) he *didn't actually believe in the supernatural.* He was a fan and follower of decidedly earthbound influences like Ayn Rand and Friedrich Nietzsche. He was not a fan of the Christian church, which he considered a corrupt cauldron of hypocrisy...a bullshit factory which proclaimed false "truths" on a platform of fear. Specifically, the fear of the devil.[220]

At the prompting of an associate, Anton LaVey decided to put a punctuation mark on his protests against Christianity (and in the promotion of his personal philosophies on life) by founding an organization named after the one mythical entity that represented the "revolutionary, creative and irrepressible spirit" within humankind.[221] After all, the advances of science and philosophy had been ripped from the teeth of antiquated Christianity. Throughout recorded history, Team Jesus had done little more than hide in its temples and under its chastity belts. It stifled learning, muted voices, preached lies, promoted guilt, instilled fear and celebrated ignorance. Conversely, Christ's adversary represented strength, progress, independence, defiance and pleasure. Satan stirred the sensory pool, drank deep and refused to stop a party when others didn't like the music. He was powerful, purposeful and unapologetic, which, in LaVey's opinion, was the true ideal for humans to aspire to. As LaVey himself would declare in his 1969 tome, "The Satanic Bible:"[222]

> *"The Satanist realizes that man, and the action and reaction of the universe, is responsible for everything, and doesn't mislead itself into thinking that someone cares. Is it not more sensible to worship a god that he, himself, has created, in accordance with his own emotional needs- one that*

220 Gilmore, Magus Peter H. "Anton Szandor LaVey". *Church of Satan.* 2015. Web.
221 Barton, Blanche. "Church of Satan History: Modern Prometheus". *Church of Satan.* 2015. Web.
222 Gilmore, Magus Peter H. "What, the Devil?". *Church of Satan.* 2015. Web.

> *best represents the very carnal and physical being that has*
> *the idea-power to invent a god in the first place?"*

If Jesus was the hand of God, Satan was a middle finger. For LaVey's purposes, he was perfect.

The Church of Satan was officially founded in 1966, and it wasn't long before a fascinated (and slightly horrified) media starting banging on LaVey's door. Anton became a memorable guest on talk shows, with his angular face, bald head, dark eyes, goatee and eerily measured cadence fueling the accusations by upstanding Christians that this former circus performer was an effigy of Satan himself. By the late 1970s, the Satanic Panic had declared Anton LaVey, his church and book an attempt by Lucifer to infect the planet. LaVey and his ilk sat back and gleefully watched the God Squad spin itself into a frothing frenzy. This Church of Satan spokesperson was the closest thing to the Antichrist that contemporary American Christians had ever seen, no doubt his presence signaling the beginning of The End.

In October of 2012, I conducted a fascinating radio interview with Peter H. Gilmore, High Priest of the Church of Satan, and he dropped a bomb that most Christians would never see coming (and most likely wouldn't accept) when he declared that the charge of Satan worship in his church is "a complete misconception. Satanism starts with *atheism*."

That's right. The Church of Satan doesn't believe in Satan.

This seems like a pretty large oversight on the part of Falwell & Friends. After all, how can LaVeyan Satanists believe in and worship the devil... if they don't believe in or worship the devil?

Now remember, Anton LaVey was a provocateur. A showman. He

was gleefully frightening doomsday preachers and blue-haired church ladies with reflections of the monster that they themselves created. He was poking at the tissue-thin skin of zealots. But he didn't believe in a literal Satan. He didn't believe in God. He didn't believe in ghosts, angels, demons, fairies, phantoms, apparitions, souls or spirits. He didn't hold to anything supernatural, and to this day, neither does his church.

So...what *does* the Church of Satan believe?

Well, essentially, the CoS is a group of flamboyant libertarians, its members described to me by Magus Gilmore as a "Halloweeny sort of folk." If I could sum up the church's Nine Satanic Statements[223] in a sentence, it would probably be: Indulge yourself, embrace life, reject stupidity, don't be weak, don't be a hypocrite, take responsibility, realize you're an animal, accept that the universe doesn't really care if you exist, and don't ever, EVER turn the other cheek. The church has other rules and guidelines, most speaking to behavior in the most libertarian sense, charging humankind to suck it up, stop whining, only give respect when another genuinely earns it, don't coddle lesser minds, know when to speak and when to shut up, and if mystical theater and ceremony help to punctuate your earthbound existence, crank up the smoke, get naked and make a party out of it.

Perhaps the most striking sentence in the Church of Satan creed is listed on its website as point #9 in "The Eleven Satanic Rules of the Earth." It says, simply, "Do not harm little children."[224] Don't harm children? How is it possible to kidnap infants, boil them in goat's blood and consume their tiny bones without harming them?

Point #10 declares, "Do not kill non-human animals unless you are

---

223 LaVey, Anton Sander. "The Nine Satanic Statements". *Church of Satan.* 1967. Web. 2015.
224 LaVey, Anton Sander. "The Eleven Satanic Rules of the Earth". *Church of Satan.* 1967. Web. 2015.

attacked, or for your food."[225] How can church members drive around neighborhoods in hearses rounding up black cats for ritual sacrifice *without harming them???*

This is a rather stunning anti-climax, no? The Church of Satan isn't a blood cult feasting on the flesh of the living and the dead to honor an actual, literal devil. It ain't Hell's kitchen. It's certainly not the damnable temple of torment we learned about on Geraldo Rivera's 1988 television special, "Exposing Satan's Underground" (a show for which Rivera later issued a public apology). Instead, it's loaded with benign, law-abiding, animal loving, atheist libertarians who like a good party. Anton LaVey's pet project is little more than a rallying point for non-religious people who think that Satan is a bigger badass than Jesus in

225 See Footnote 224.

Christian mythology, who focus inward rather than upward, who want to extract the marrow from each moment, who think the meek will get steamrolled while waiting to inherit the earth, and who think it's hysterical fun to waltz up to God's flock, peer down over the fences at the sheep and say, "BOO!"

I can't believe I'm admitting this, but I have more in common with the Church of Satan than I do the protestant Baptist and Pentecostal churches of my youth. I'm not really CoS material, though, as I'm decidedly not a "Halloweeny sort of folk," I think an inward focus should be complemented with attention and compassion toward others, and I part ways with LaVeyan philosophy that the weak should be dominated by the strong. I'm all about the individual, but I'm also about helping the less fortunate and disadvantaged.

Like all churches, there are many spinoffs and denominations related to Satanism, and some actually do hold to the spiritual forces of Light and Dark. There are theistic Satanists, gnostic Satanists, Luciferians, Palladists, Detians, Demonolators, etc, each incarnation having its own unique scriptures, codes, philosophies and cultures. But in regard the official Church of Satan, the idiom proves true: the devil is not so black as he is painted.

Perhaps it's time for a generation of clucking church hens to unruffle their feathers, base any protests in actual facts and take a clue from those who fear Satan as much as they fear Lord Voldemort.

Perhaps it's time to give the devil his due.

CHAPTER 19
This is the End (Beautiful Friend)

If many world religions have one thing in common (and you've probably seen the trend in this book), it's that they await some kind of apocalyptic Final Chapter, and they're not speaking about the point in time, 2.8 billion years from now, when our sun's naturally-rising temperature transforms Earth into a giant George Foreman Grill. No, they foresee some other agent whose primary mission is to punch the human ticket. Permanently.

I became interested in these types of predictions during the days of Y2K: The Millennium Bug.

Up to that time, personal, business and military computers implemented a simple two-digit date code, until someone finally woke up and realized that the year 2000 might suddenly confuse computer programs into thinking they were operating decades before the Great Depression. There were serious fears that we'd see a global shutdown of critical systems, the corruption of financial records, dropped security protocols, erased databanks and the collapse of civilization as we knew it.

As soon as the issue hit the news networks, the public did what the public does: it freaked. Panicked people immediately began stockpiling canned food, moving cash out of banks and into mattresses, stocking their survival kits, and even amassing weapons. Alarmist Y2K books popped up almost overnight. Religious windbags like Jerry Falwell, Pat Robertson, James Dobson and D. James Kennedy warned of the End of Days depicted in the biblical book of Revelation. Falwell himself went on national television to personally scare the crap out of the public (and also offer for sale his handy Y2K video, "A Christian's Guide to the Millennium Bug").

Of course, outside of a few bumps, January 1st, 2000 rang in smoothly, the bug was deftly handled by clever programmers and, ironically, Y2K became an anticlimax of near biblical proportions. Speaking of the Bible, the Reverend Falwell apologized to his viewers for the mistake and happily refunded the mountains of cash he made on those $28-per-unit VHS tapes.

Of course, I'm lying. Ol' Jerry kept the cash and slithered back to his lair, perhaps stuffing his own mattress with the spoils.

Few people know about the disaster predicted to occur only five months *after* Y2K. A few years before the millennium, a guy named

Richard Noone had penned the book, "5/5/2000 Ice: the Ultimate Disaster," which (thanks to handy info gleaned from hugely credible sources like the Great Pyramid, freemasons and the Illuminati) warned that Mercury, Venus, Mars, Jupiter and Saturn would align with the Earth in a way that caused the polar ice caps to melt and initiate a catastrophic, global flood.[226] I recently did a "This Day in History" search for 5/5/2000 and found no earth-shattering news beyond the marriage of Angelina Jolie to Billy Bob Thornton, which to many of us at the time, did actually seem like a sign of apocalyptic doom.

Warnings like these are actually nothing new. Recorded history is a Greatest Hits of failed doomsday predictions. Early Romans believed that twelve eagles had revealed the date that their great city (and civilization) would be destroyed: 634 BCE.[227] Hippolytus, the 3rd century theologian, predicted that Christ would return only 500 years after his resurrected body ascended to Heaven.[228] Pope Sylvester II announced that The End would occur on January 1, 1000, the end of the first millennium.[229] Pope Innocent III (yeah, "Innocent" was his chosen Pope name) continued the Catholic tradition of screwing the predictive pooch by declaring that the world would end 666 years after the rise of Islam, or 1284 CE.[230] Many 13th Century Europeans saw the black plague as a signal that the world was ending. Martin Luther didn't think we'd last past the year 1600.[231] John Wesley, founder of the Methodists, interpreted the words of Revelation

226 Noone, Richard W. *5/5/2000: Ice- The Ultimate Disaster, Revised Edition*. New York: Three Rivers Press. 1997. Print.
227 Thompson, Damian. *The End of Time: Faith and Fear in the Shadow of the Millennium*. Hanover, New Hampshire: University Press of New England. 1997. p. 19. Print.
228 "The Prophetic Faith of our Fathers" Froom, LeRoy (1950).
229 Boyett, Jason. *Pocket Guide to the Apocalypse: The Official Field Manual for the End of the World*. Winter Park, Florida: Relevant Media Group. 2005. Print.
230 Lazarus, William P. and Sullivan, Mark. *Comparative Religion for Dummies*. Hoboken, New Jeresy: John Wiley & Sons. 2008. p. 237. Print.
231 Weber, Eugen. *Apocalypses*. Cambridge MA: Harvard University Press. 1999. Print.

12:14 to mean that Christ would return in 1836.[232] Charles Taze Russell, one of the foundational icons of the Jehovah's Witnesses, pinned 1914 on his apocalyptic calendar.[233] Herbert W. Armstrong, founder of the Worldwide Church of God, made no less than *four* End Of Days predictions (1936, 1943, 1972 and 1975) and blew all of them.[234]

Christian author Hal Lindsey (and co-author C.C. Carlson) jumped on the Revelation bandwagon with his 1970 book, "The Late, Great Planet Earth." No actual date for the End was given (Lindsey was smart enough not to paint himself into a corner), but as the book sold over 35 million copies and was turned into a feature film, I'm guessing Hal is rooting for more royalty checks to arrive before the appearance of the Blood Moon and the sound of the Trumpet. After all, a guy who has been married four times obviously has significant financial responsibilities[235] (I do wonder if Hal Lindsey's powers of "sight" might have prevented some poor relationship choices).

And of course, as 21st century readers, we can't talk about the apocalypse without at least a brief mention of the infamous pastor, Harold Camping. The 50-year president of Family Radio, Camping capped a lifetime of failed End Times prognostications with a hugely well-funded advertising campaign predicting that May 21, 2011 would be Judgment Day. He apparently pulled (from his ass) Christian scriptures containing the correct equations and calculations, and then he set off to warn 7 billion earthly inhabitants that the Christian Rapture was written in permanent red ink on God's divine daytimer. Thousands of billboards were erected worldwide. Public benches were branded with instructions to "Save the Date." Vehicles

---

232 McIver, Tom. *The End of the World: An Annotated Bibliography*. Jefferson, NC: McFarlane & Co. 1999. Print.

233 Cohen, Daniel. *Prophets of Doom*. Brookfield, CT: The Millbrook Press, Inc. 1999. Print.

234 Shaw, Eva. *Eve of Destruction*. Los Angeles: Lowell House. 1995. Print.

235 "The Who's Who of Prophecy". *Rapture Ready*. 2015. Web.

toured city streets wrapped in scriptures from Ezekiel, Proverbs and Revelation, warning all passers-by that "The Bible Guarantees It." The media gladly boosted ratings by parading Harold Camping and his minions across our television screens. The whole world waited on the razor's edge!

When the faithful saw May 21, 2011 pass without incident and knocked on the front door of Family Radio headquarters that weekend seeking an explanation, the only response was the note pasted on the window: "This office is closed. Sorry we missed you."[236] ("Sorry we missed you" should be the default slogan for every End Times prediction in recorded history.)

I suppose we shouldn't be too hard on the late Harold Camping (he died in December 2013...of natural causes). After all, even Jesus Christ's prediction about his own return was an epic fail, as he told his disciples in Matthew 16 that some of them would witness the "Son of Man coming in his Kingdom" before they died.

And then, within a few years, all of the disciples...died.

This Second Coming has been, well, a long time coming, and as humankind has held its collective breath for 21 centuries, the most recent signs and sightings have been limited to vague eyewitness claims and the miraculous manifestations of Christ's image in cloud formations and on perishable foods. We have Burned Toast Jesus. Fish Stick Jesus. Banana Peel Jesus. Kit Kat Jesus. Cheeto Jesus. Greasy Frying Pan Jesus. Mold Stain Jesus. Peeled Potato Jesus. Tree Stump Jesus. Pretzel Jesus. Grilled Cheese Sandwich Jesus. And, most embarrassingly, Dog's Anus Jesus (which does bear a striking resemblance to those kitschy oil paintings found in many churches).

---

236 Eversley, Melanie. "Apocalypse some other time". *USA Today*. 22 May 2011. Web.

Perhaps a clue to this mysterious absence can be gleaned from Matthew 24:36, where Christ declared his own ignorance on this whole Second Coming thing: "But about that day or hour no one knows, not even the angels in heaven, nor the Son, but only the Father." Of course, Christ also declared that "I and the Father are one" (John 10:30), meaning that Jesus would be keeping the secret...from himself. (Perhaps it's a left-brain / right-brain thing.)

There have been plenty who've pounded the End Times drum that weren't aligned with a mainstream deity or church. Astrologers, seers, forecasters, prophets, psychics, shamans and soothsayers have a long history of finding messages in the stars, in the cards, in the crystals, in the bones, in the asylum of their own wild imaginations. If you remember, the Mayan Apocalypse arrived with a loud, dull thud in December 2012, despite all of the bombast about asteroids, supernovas and aliens. That same period saw the first experiments of the Large

Hadron Collider, its particle-smashing search for the Higgs-Boson almost certainly destined to create an earth-sucking black hole. (Had this occurred, it would have made Peter Higgs' 2013 Nobel Prize for Physics a bit more challenging.) For thousands of years, the prophets of doom have been climbing to the tops of the highest cliffs and shouting about gods, goddesses, asteroids, planets, volcanoes, calendars, codes, equations, signs, revelations and the fiery curtain that will close upon us all, and *nobody* has gotten it right.

Will this knowledge inoculate us from being taken in by the next doomsday quack? I think we both know the answer.

But perhaps there's something else at work here. Perhaps our obsession with the threats Out There provides a convenient equivocation for and distraction from the legitimate and serious threats Down Here: earthquakes, hurricanes, floods, avalanches, droughts, eclipses, famine, poverty, disease, terrorism, war, genocide, etc. We have difficulty processing these overwhelming events, so we do what our ancient ancestors did in their moments of ignorance and awe: we draw the outline of another agency at work. Something larger than us. Smarter than us. Stronger than us. Something that is in control. And even if it arrives with evil intent, at least this cosmic iron fist is in charge and has a playbook. In our helplessness, we find that knowledge comforting.

A December 2012 article in Scientific American explored research done by University of Minnesota neuroscientist Shmuel Lissek, an expert on fear, and Lissek's data seems to back this up. Doomsday mythology allows humans to relinquish power, and it also absolves us of personal responsibility. Of course, people react to the concept of inevitability in wildly different ways. News of an approaching killer asteroid might send one person off to his steel-encased bomb shelter and another person to Key West with a cold brew and a lawn chair, but both cases enjoy the rare luxury of certainty.[237] Que Sera, Sera. Whatever will be, will be.

There might also be a pleasure element to the equation. Perhaps we enjoy being frightened, like ticket-buying patrons of a haunted house willing to suspend rationality for a few scares and inject some adrenaline-fueled drama into our humdrum routines. We emerge uninjured from the exit door, share a few euphoric laughs about the experience and move on. Maybe the blood moon, killer asteroid and the Mayan calendar are just thrill rides, the sense-assaulting contraptions of traveling carnivals which happily fuel their wares on the wide eyes and open wallets of an eager public.

---

237   Yuhas, Daisy. "Psychology Reveals the Comforts of the Apocalypse". *Scientific American*. 18 December 2012. Web.

Regardless, it's a foregone conclusion that we'll continue to see the failed predictions of the Bad News Club, and we'll subsequently find their alarmist books and videos in retail bargain bins, coated in dust and cleverly hidden under a small, hand-written sign that says, "Sorry we missed you."

Afterword

Before we say goodbye, I wanted to thank you for reading this book. For authors (or creators of any stripe), sophomore efforts are a dicey and often calamitous affair. While it did incorporate a measure of lightheartedness and humor, my first book, "Deconverted: a Journey from Religion to Reason," was a somewhat serious, autobiographical chronicle of my journey out of fundamentalist Christianity. With "Sacred Cows," I wanted to lighten things up with a playful romp through the often religiously and culturally imposed edicts and practices far beyond my former faith, hopefully leaving the reader with a few interesting morsels of information, a brief distraction from the chaos of everyday life, and a smile.

If I'm to lay all of my cards on the table, I must also admit that I've displayed these often humorous snapshots of rotes and rituals with an agenda...a desire to examine the human condition in a larger context.

Certainly, some of our traditions and behaviors are beautiful and even beneficial, enhancing the human experience and stoking the fires of both the individual and the tribe. We've constructed countless opportunities to stand out and/or to blend in. We act, react, create, modify, color, recite, dismantle, build and share as temporary beings bent on finding meaning and purpose, maximizing our tiny but unique footprints upon this earth. And as someone who has recently opened his eyes to the larger canvas of beauty out there, I often feel I'm discovering the world anew every single day.

In that context, I think traditions aren't just disposable accessories to our existence, but instead can provide frames to border the rich portraits of life experience, and the beliefs which drive those traditions can find their roots in rationality without rendering us slaves. If I may quote W. Somerset Maugham, "Tradition is a guide and not a jailer."

Perhaps a less cryptic summation comes from that popular internet photo of a man who signed up for Spain's Running of the Bulls and found himself scrambling to escape an ivory enema. The caption reads, "Just because you've always done it that way doesn't mean it's not incredibly stupid."

To bring the conversation full circle, let's again look at how all of our antics might appear to the extraterrestrial I mentioned in this book's introduction. Peering through his telescope, the alien observes supposedly higher primates who are convinced that a full, secure, happy, meaningful life requires that they blow billows of smoke toward the clouds, toss goats, spin dogs, whack the heads from unsuspecting chickens, dance with serpents, rub against turtles, consult crystals, don enchanted garments and seek wisdom hidden inside fortune cookies.

As the subjects of his study, we burn the sacred incense. We ingest the communion wine. We stare into crystal balls. We caress our talismans. We roll the bones. We shout, faint, and are revived to faint again. We are the slapstick comedy on which the curtain never seems to fall.

Does a purposeful, rich, physically and mentally healthy life really require us to fumble so? When the sun sets on our puerile prayers and practices, do we really think our petitions have kept the stars in their proper alignment? Will we ever stop, look, listen and ultimately laugh at ourselves for being the pratfalling victims of our own superstitious joke? Can we summon the strength to decide that we don't require a magical bauble chained around our necks, but can create good fortune, good medicine, good deeds, good times and goodwill through decision and action anchored in the real world?

Will we come to the realization that ideas aren't guaranteed respect (even the ones deemed untouchable by the prophets and priests), that any respect given must be earned daily through careful scrutiny and testing, and that by casting off our fearful and superstitious shackles, we can exchange blissful ignorance for a genuine, gratifying, priceless freedom?

Will we kick open the gate and release our sacred cows?

Only time will tell.

Until that day, I wish for you a life rich with love, laughter, grand encounters, tender moments, helping hands, fond memories, and perhaps most importantly, the freedom to see past and break through the restrictive walls that others attempt to build around you.

They may find comfort inside the fences, but you were born to be free.

∽o∾

END

∽o∾

194

Also By The Author

Audio book version of "Sacred Cows: a Lighthearted Look at Belief and Tradition Around the World" (read by the author)

"Deconverted: a Journey from Religion to Reason"

CPSIA information can be obtained
at www.ICGtesting.com
Printed in the USA
FSOW04n1217150615
7926FS